CORPORATE FINANCE

C000075913

MERGERS AND ACQUISITIONS

A FRAMEWORK FOR THE RIGHT EXECUTIVE DECISION

Dr Hazel Johnson

FINANCIAL TIMES

PRENTICE HALL

PEARSON EDUCATION LIMITED

Head Office:
Edinburgh Gate
Harlow CM20 2JE
Tel: +44 (0)1279 623623
Fax: +44 (0)1279 431059

London Office:
128 Long Acre, London WC2E 9AN
Tel: +44 (0)171 447 2000
Fax: +44 (0)171 240 5771

First published in Great Britain in 1999

© Pearson Education Limited 1999

The right of Dr Hazel Johnson to be identified as
Author of this Work has been asserted by her in accordance
with the Copyright, Designs, and Patent Act 1988.

ISBN 0 273 63881 5

British Library Cataloguing in Publication Data
A CIP catalogue record for this book can be obtained
from the British Library.

All rights reserved; no part of this publication may be reproduced,
stored in a retrieval system, or transmitted in any form or by any means,
electronic, mechanical, photocopying, recording, or otherwise without either
the prior written permission of the Publishers or a licence permitting restricted
copying in the United Kingdom issued by the Copyright Licensing Agency Ltd,
90 Tottenham Court Road, London W1P 0LP. This book may not be lent,
resold, hired out or otherwise disposed of by way of trade in any form
of binding or cover other than that in which it is published,
without the prior consent of the Publishers.

1 3 5 7 9 10 8 6 4 2

Typeset by Northern Phototypesetting Co Ltd.
Printed and bound in Great Britain by
Redwood Books, Trowbridge, Wiltshire.

*The Publishers' policy is to use paper manufactured
from sustainable forests.*

ABOUT THE AUTHOR

Dr Hazel J. Johnson is Distinguished University Scholar at the University of Louisville and Professor of Finance (USA). Dr Johnson was formerly a member of the finance faculty of Georgetown University (Washington, DC, USA). She has authored more than 20 books in the areas of international finance and financial institutions. With publications in the USA, Europe, Latin America, and Asia, Dr Johnson's work has been translated into Japanese and Spanish. In addition, she has developed software systems for business practitioners in the areas of bank valuation, capital budgeting, cost of capital, and mergers and acquisitions. Dr Johnson has acted as a consultant to more than 50 major US financial institutions and a number of state and federal agencies.

In loving memory of Ida W. Kelly
and Lucille V. Johnson.

CONTENTS

Contents

FOREWORD

Making decisions concerning mergers and acquisitions is both science and art. In consolidating two separate companies, issues of strategy, price, and corporate culture must come together in one coherent analysis of the new combined firm.

Mergers and Acquisitions: A Framework for the Right Executive Decision brings together the science and the art. First, a company must establish the right reasons to merge with another firm or to acquire a business. Being a larger company after a merger is, in itself, not a good reason to merge. Instead, the firm's strategic plan and direction should drive the decision. Selecting the appropriate merger partner or acquisition target involves many factors, including products, customers, costs, corporate culture, and human resources considerations.

In some cases, other means of collaborating with a firm may be more advantageous than merger. Some of these alternatives are joint ventures, strategic alliances, minority investments, venture capital activities, or licensing arrangements. In other cases, managers must decide whether the firm should be sold to another company.

When merger *is* the right decision and the right partner has been identified, the business combination will fail unless the right price is associated with the transaction. Valuation methods are based on sound theoretical concepts. However, considerable judgment is required to project appropriate cash flows.

The accompanying *Mergers and Acquisitions Firm Valuation Software System* helps bring all the concepts together in a smooth transition from theory to practice. The Excel 7.0 based system facilitates a discounted cash flow (DCF) valuation of a commercial enterprise. Cash flows are projected for a five-year period and a terminal value is estimated to capture the value of cash flows after the forecasted period. Individual schedules detail projected operational cash flows, including a highly specific range of expenses; working capital changes; projected capital expenditures; and tax benefits associated with depreciation and amortization. Cash flow analysis and firm valuation are performed automatically.

Mergers and Acquisitions: A Framework for the Right Executive Decision answers three critical questions:

- When should a firm consider a merger or acquisition?
- How should a firm structure its acquisition team and approach?
- How does a firm determine the right price for a merger partner or acquisition target?

Together the book and the software provide structure and support for one of the most important decisions of the firm.

CHAPTER 1

CONCEPTUAL ISSUES SURROUNDING MERGERS AND ACQUISITIONS

Introduction

■

The Growing Merger Trend in Europe

■

Business Combination Philosophies

■

Structural Aspects of Mergers and Acquisitions

■

Valuation Concepts

■

Valuation Methodologies

■

Avoiding Mishaps

INTRODUCTION

In Europe, the philosophical shift toward greater private control of corporations has led to new thinking on the part of corporate decision makers. Michael Zaoui, co-head of European M&A at Morgan Stanley in Europe recently remarked:

Every single chief executive should ask themselves whether their company can survive without actively considering and pursuing a business combination...[1]

In terms of analyzing the direction of a particular industry, another market participant, Hugh Scott-Barrett, chief executive of European corporate finance at ABN Amro in London, noted:

Arguably, one should be looking at the industry more from a perspective of what it will look like in the future, rather than the way in which it's been perceived in the past.[2]

THE GROWING MERGER TREND IN EUROPE

Factors Contributing to the Trend

European merger transactions are being propelled by several economic and political forces that have developed in the last 10 to 15 years.

- Globalization has had major implications for industrial competitiveness – lowering the cost of labor and opening markets to a greater number of producing firms.
- Financial markets have become more integrated – facilitating cross-border financial transactions related to business combinations and other business activities.

---

[1] See Brewis, J. and Drexhage, G. (1998) "M&A Boom Reverberates Around the World," *Corporate Finance*, 31–35.
[2] Ibid.

- Privatization of previously state-owned enterprises has encouraged business combinations across public and private sectors.
- The Single European Market has expanded the potential horizon of virtually every company.
- Economic and monetary union in Europe has lowered the real and perceived barriers to business throughout Europe.
- The promise of Eastern European countries as participants in the European integration process adds fuel to the expansion fires.
- Recessionary conditions in Europe have forced greater attention to competitive issues – some of which can be addressed through cost-cutting business combinations.

These forces have become extremely powerful and are acting to counterbalance historical business patterns in Europe – especially continental Europe. The historical patterns have included:

- close control of corporations;
- nonmarket valuation of shares transferred;
- corporate control through minority positions in a large network of stakeholdings;
- resistance to hostile takeovers, leveraged buyouts, and the advice of independent advisers.

Now, change is being effected through a variety of regulatory reforms in national markets and at the European Union level – change that will increase the efficiency of the marketplace.

Minority Stakes versus Full Ownership

In the meantime, the dynamics of minority stakeholding in Europe warrant some attention. In the ten years ended 1995, transactions that involved a transfer of partial ownership were a much larger percentage of total merger and acquisition activity in continental Europe than in the USA or the UK. Classifying the transactions by the domicile of the firm being acquired, the following are the percentages of partial ownership transactions for the 10-year period:

- United States – 13.7 percent
- United Kingdom – 24.0 percent
- rest of Europe – 35.0 percent.

There are several apparent reasons that European firms are more likely to be involved in a partial-ownership deal.

- A strategic alliance permits two companies to pursue a common objective without relinquishing independence.
- A gradual commitment to a final arrangement is wiser, cheaper, and reversible.
- In many cases, a substantial minority stakeholding can assure effective control of a company.

The proclivity for partial stakeholding in Europe is in contrast to a general preference for 100 percent ownership in the USA. US acquirers often prefer total ownership because of tax, accounting, and legal considerations. For example, pooling of interests of two firms combines the companies in a tax-free transaction. Also, eliminating minority interests in firms also reduces the likelihood of lawsuits on behalf of minority shareholders.

Some observers suggest that lengthy European alliances or "trial marriages," may lead to full mergers that are more lasting and beneficial than the more impulsive, opportunistic US acquisitions. Often, the latter appear to fail to deliver expected benefits. Nevertheless, minority investments have shortcomings. In many instances, for example, the seller of the stake seeks to preserve a relationship that is actually economically inefficient. Also, strategic alliances – perhaps involving a 10 percent cross-shareholding between two competing companies from different countries – may appear shrewd when announced but fail to produce the intended synergies. Within a few years, each company may find itself unable to influence policies in the company to which it is allied and may be in serious competition with it.

Thus, mergers and acquisitions in Europe are increasing. Competitive factors are likely to lead to more 100-percent-ownership changes in the future.

BUSINESS COMBINATION PHILOSOPHIES

A vision of the firm in combination with another can take a variety of forms. Inevitably, there can be several reasons for a business combination as well as a variety of anticipated benefits from the combination of two firms. Acquisition of an ongoing business implies the purchase of a set of income-generating resources. In any event, the following questions should be addressed.

- Is an acquisition more cost-effective than internal development? The price paid must be lower than the total resources necessary for internal development of a comparable strategic outcome.
- What expertise is being acquired and how productive will it be?
- Do the anticipated benefits reflect significant future value?
- Can meaningful synergies be developed between the two companies? This is an issue that goes far beyond a valuation of the assets and liabilities listed on the balance sheet.

The philosophy of a merger or acquisition can follow a portfolio strategy, a business family strategy, or a business element strategy.

The Portfolio Strategy

The objective of the portfolio strategy is to develop a set of interrelated businesses that provide reasonable balance and stability within the firm. The diversification of businesses may be developed purely on financial principles. That is, the two businesses may produce cash flows that are not perfectly correlated, producing more stable combined cash flows. Alternatively, the portfolio may be constructed by joining businesses that, to some degree, are related in terms of technology, industry expertise, or product-market niches – that is, nonfinancial considerations. In the case of nonfinancial portfolio strategy, the business combination will focus on interrelationships among the businesses, perhaps an essential or core skill to support the firm. Planning for an acquisition in this context involves a search for business entities that will balance and strengthen the firm's position.

1

The Business Family Strategy

The business family strategy attempts to create synergies that actually grow the business opportunities beyond the current level for the two individual firms. Closely related businesses can build on a common technology or base of expertise as it applies to the acquirer's business practices. The acquisition is used to develop related new business activities. The business family strategy yields a group of interrelated businesses that allow the firm to exploit shared resources in technology, product markets, or distribution channels, and to build new businesses from the foundations of existing units. Combinations may be driven by the need to enter new growth markets.

The Business Element Strategy

The business element strategy addresses the issue of a direct competitor for capturing a particular customer. Success depends on developing competitive strength in a specific business segment. An acquisition under this strategy may be a means to a greater market share by takeover of a competitor. Potentially, such a combination can strengthen the firm's internal operations by expanding its product and/or service lines while simultaneously reducing competition.

STRUCTURAL ASPECTS OF MERGERS AND ACQUISITIONS

Whatever the philosophy of a business combination, there are certain structural approaches to a merger or acquisition. In strategic planning, a firm must decide which of these three philosophies it is pursuing and then determine how a combination may further its plan.[3] The structure should be adopted that will accomplish objectives associated with either the portfolio, business family, or business element philosophy. But within that guideline, there are several different types of combinations, just as there are different philosophical approaches. The structural forms of acquisitions may be classified as horizontal, vertical, concentric, or unrelated (conglomerate) combinations.

Horizontal Combinations

In horizontal combinations, one firm acquires another firm in the same industry. The principal anticipated benefits from this type of combination are economies of scale in production and distribution, and possible increases in market power in a more concentrated industry. The primary impetus for strategic analysis of a horizontal acquisition would originate with a business element philosophy. Benefits to the acquirer would be primarily in the form of a strengthened product-market strategic position.

Vertical Combinations

In vertical combinations, the two firms are in industries with strong supplier-buyer relationships. The acquired firm is either a supplier or a customer of the acquiring firm. A vertical acquisition usually is undertaken when the market for the intermediate product is imperfect, because of scarcity of resources, criticality of the purchased products, or control over production specifications of the intermediate product, among other

---

[3] See Chapter 2 for a description of the strategic planning process and using the strategic plan to identify potential business partners.

reasons. Reasons for vertical combination may be consistent with either the business element philosophy or the business family philosophy. At the business element level, vertical acquisitions that give a competitive advantage in terms of cost might be considered. At the business family level, acquisitions that benefit a group of businesses (and have transferable and broader resources) might be proposed.

Concentric Combinations

In a concentric combination, the two firms are related through basic technologies, production processes, or markets. The acquired firm represents an extension of the product lines, market participations, or technologies of the acquiring firm. Essentially, such combinations are geared to expansion and are consistent with the business family philosophy. Concentric combinations expand the scope of the acquiring firm by establishing a presence in contiguous businesses. Benefits could be derived from economics of scope (exploitation of a shared resource) and, ideally, from entry into a related market having higher returns than the acquirer formerly enjoyed.

The potential benefits are high because these acquisitions offer opportunities to diversify around a common core of strategic resources. Concentric acquisitions can affect different business families in the acquiring firm. Thus, the primary planning for these combinations should be at the parent company level, to promote a unifying theme among the firm's entities.

Unrelated or Conglomerate Combinations

Unrelated or conglomerate combinations are not explicitly based on sharing resources, technologies, synergies, or product-market strategies. Instead, the focus is on how the acquired entity can enhance the overall stability and balance of the firm's total portfolio. Strategic analysis for conglomerate combinations must be done at the corporate level. These combinations are consistent with the portfolio philosophy.

VALUATION CONCEPTS

After the broad strategic issues have been addressed, the business combination must be valued. That is, the price must be determined.

The process of valuing a prospective merger partner or acquisition target involves both quantitative and qualitative issues. At the core of valuation lies the institution's balance sheet – the assets and liabilities that represent future cash flows. Increasingly, the rights and obligations that are not recorded on the balance sheet have assumed a more significant role – swaps, forward contracts, and other option-like instruments. In addition, unfunded pension liabilities can represent significant amounts.

Of course, the future revenues and expenses are an essential part of the valuation process. Exactly how these future cash flow streams are analyzed depends on the valuation philosophy that is adopted. Several concepts are possible:

- intrinsic value
- acquisition value
- liquidation and replacement value.

Each of these concepts contribute to the analysis of the price to be paid.

Intrinsic Value

Intrinsic financial value captures the discounted present value of the free cash flows generated by the assets of a business as a going concern plus a terminal value of the business, also discounted to the present at an appropriate discount rate. Thus, intrinsic valuation is based on a time series of financial flows.

The discounted cash flow (DCF) methodology is used to implement this valuation concept. The methodology is based on assumptions concerning the nature of cash flows and the appropriate rate at which to find the present value of the cash flows. The calculated intrinsic value of the company, thus, changes as the assumptions change.

As is true in most analyses, a DCF valuation is only as good as the assumptions or projections on which it is based. The projections always must be subjected to a test of reasonableness. One of the most exacting tests of reasonableness is to compare the historical performance of the company on certain key financial measures (e.g. rate of growth, profit margins, capital intensity) to the forecasted performance. A forecast that, for example, projects dramatic improvements in margins must be investigated further before being accepted at face value. As a further test for reasonableness, historical and projected financial performance of the company being valued should be compared to the performance of the industry or other companies in the industry.

Acquisition Value

The acquisition value of a company is the price at which the company would trade in the market for corporate control and may differ significantly from its intrinsic financial value. Thus, acquisition value is the price that an acquirer would pay to control the free cash flows of the targeted firm. It should be noted that merger and acquisition transactions often occur at prices significantly above market values in the secondary trading market for the stock.

Investment bankers continually conduct public and private auctions for firms that attract a number of bidders. These contests in the market for corporate control can be highly competitive and, accordingly, should accurately reflect value.

Also, acquisition value of a firm in combination with another firm may be different from the value of the firm in isolation. The acquisition value will reflect incremental cash flows attributable to consolidated tax savings, costs savings tied to elimination of redundant operations, distribution economics, or other such synergies. Of course, synergy can be an elusive goal because realization of synergies is much more difficult to achieve than identification of them. Nevertheless, if synergy is defined as incremental increases in free cash flow that occur as a direct result of the business combination, these increases should be reflected in the value of the merger or acquisition.

Liquidation and Replacement Value

Other concepts of value include liquidation value and replacement value. Liquidation value forms a floor on the value of the firm. This concept of value is an estimate of the net proceeds (after expenses) of selling the assets of the company at their fair market value and satisfying all liabilities, including taxes associated with the liquidation. Some estimate of the time required to liquidate the assets must also be developed.

Replacement value of the firm is the cost of duplicating the assets of the firm at current costs. This concept of value is of interest in evaluating the alternatives of either

- acquiring the assets in question by acquiring another firm or
- building the asset base *de novo* (from the ground up) or expanding existing assets internally.

VALUATION METHODOLOGIES

For purposes of mergers and acquisitions, the value of a company is often operationalized in terms of book value, assets minus liabilities – or more precisely, some multiple of book value. There are several practical methodologies of valuation, most notably:

- discounted cash flow (DCF)
- P/E valuation
- adjusted book value.

These methodologies reflect the valuation concepts of intrinsic value and acquisition value.

Discounted Cash Flow (DCF)

The discounted cash flow (DCF) approach is the most theoretically valid approach because it considers future cash flow streams and the appropriate market rates to apply to them in determining market value. In the USA, this approach has been stipulated by the Financial Accounting Standards Board (FASB) as the correct method of fair market valuation when objective quotations are unavailable.[4] In the application of DCF techniques to firm valuation, it is frequently assumed that earnings represent a good approximation of cash flow. A growth rate of earnings for the near term is also specified and earnings adjustments are made, as applicable. An example of an earnings adjustment is removing the effect of large amortizations of goodwill (from previous acquisitions).

The process of DCF valuation often consists of the following steps.

1 Project earnings for each of the next five years, individually.
2 Find the present value of each year's earnings with the appropriate discount factor, using a weighted average cost of capital.
3 Apply a P/E ratio to the earnings in year 6 to establish the value of all earnings after year 5.
4 Find the present value of the result in step 3, using a discount factor for five years.

The advantage of this process is that it incorporates sound principles of financial theory with the use of present value factors. However, there are several disadvantages as follows.

■ The use of one discount rate assumes a constant capital structure and constant cost of capital. Actually, the capital structure will change whenever the firm issues debt, but not equity, and vice versa. Also, the cost of capital can change whenever general economic conditions change, changing the required rate of return for debt and equity.

---

[4] For example, FASB has indicated the use of DCF in connection with required market value disclosures (SFAS No. 107) and measurement of loan impairment (SFAS No. 114).

- The use of one growth rate for the earnings stream in the first five years assumes that the mix of business activities will remain the same. This can be an unrealistic assumption, particularly if new products are under development.
- Multiplying earnings in year 6 by a given P/E ratio is equivalent to dividing the earnings by the E/P ratio which, in turn, is equivalent to capitalizing the earnings at a rate of return that is required by equity holders in a no-growth scenario. Unless it is assumed that there will be no growth after year 5, this is inappropriate.

Nevertheless, if adjustments are made for these factors, the DCF methodology is far superior to other approaches often used, notably P/E valuation and adjusted book value.

P/E Valuation

P/E valuation is a subset of the DCF process, as it is commonly applied. This methodology involves:

1 finding a comparable company whose stock is publicly traded;
2 determining the P/E ratio of the publicly traded firm;
3 multiplying the earnings of the firm being analyzed by the P/E ratio of the publicly traded company.

The approach is simple and intuitively appealing. However, the disadvantages are several.

- As indicated in the discussion of DCF methodology, this approach assumes no growth in earnings.
- If the stock in the company being analyzed is not also publicly traded, its illiquidity will cause an over-valuation.
- It is difficult to find a truly comparable, publicly traded firm because of differences in competition, asset mix, management, and other variables.

The P/E valuation approach is probably best used as a first pass at valuation or to test for reasonableness the result of a more detailed valuation.

Adjusted Book Value

The adjusted book value approach attempts to compensate for those factors that cause the book value of equity to differ from the market value. Book value is commonly adjusted by:

1 subtracting intangibles (goodwill, patents, and copyrights);

2 adding to the value of property, plant, and equipment, as appropriate;

3 writing off questionable receivables ("haircuts");

4 marking to market any securities that have been recorded at cost;

5 recognizing the impact of any upcoming maturity of debt, its associated payoff, and the affect of refunding;

6 adding significant unfunded pension liabilities to the liabilities of the firm;

7 making any other adjustments to the balance sheet that appear warranted.

This approach is useful, but rarely can be considered a complete valuation for at least two reasons.

■ Off-balance-sheet financial positions are ignored (forward contracts, swap arrangements, or futures positions).

■ Profit-generating activities of the firm (revenues and expenses) are not valued in any way.

Like P/E valuation, adjusted book value is most appropriately used as a test for reasonableness in the context of a more detailed valuation.

AVOIDING MISHAPS

Both a logical rationale for a business combination and a reasonable valuation are essential if a merger or acquisition is to be considered successful. Such decisions can profoundly change the nature of a company. Careful analysis and attention to detail will help ensure that the change is not accompanied by unpleasant surprises, but instead, elevates the market position of the two merging entities.

Selected References

Celarier, M. (December 1997) "Europe's Takeover Boom Gathers Pace," *Euromoney*, 66–68.

Brewis, J. and Drexhage, G. (April 1998) "M&A Boom Reverberates Around the World," *Corporate Finance*, 31–35.

Rock, M. L., Rock, R. H., and Sikora, M. (1994) *The Mergers & Acquisitions Handbook*. 2nd edn. New York: McGraw-Hill.

Smith, R. C. (1993) *Comeback: The Restoration of Banking Power in the New World Economy*. Boston, Massachusetts: Harvard Business School Press.

Smith, R. C. and Walter, I. (1997) *Global Banking*. New York: Oxford University Press.

MERGERS

INTRODUCTION

A merger is a combination of two or more organizations through pooling of common stock, cash payment to the company being acquired, or a combination of the two. In mergers, management of the two companies typically consent. Chief executive officers (CEOs) are continuously discussing the next potential merger partner, with many questions surrounding this issue.

- When is the right time to merge?
- How do you identify the right partner?
- How do you successfully communicate the benefits of the merger?
- How do you approach consolidating the two firms?

THE RIGHT TIME TO MERGE

In order to assess the right time to merge, each company must identify its strategic direction after thoroughly analyzing its strengths, weaknesses, opportunities, and threats (SWOT). The process contains the elements noted in Figure 2.1:

FIGURE 2.1

The Foundation for Deciding the Right Time to Merge

- The Company's Mission
- Industry Analysis
- Analysis of Strengths, Weaknesses, Opportunities, and Threats
- The Firm's Strategic Plan

- defining the firm's mission
- performing an industry analysis
- conducting a SWOT analysis
- crafting a strategic plan.

The Mission Statement

A mission statement defines the firm's overall reason for being, its role in the community in which it operates, and perhaps its style of management. This statement is typically a two- to three-paragraph document that reflects the culture of the institution and its focus. The two overriding questions that the mission statement will answer are: "Who are we?" and "Why are we here?" The mission statement is necessarily concise because it must capture sentiments that can be shared by every employee of the company.

The Industry Analysis

The purpose of the industry analysis is to survey the industry in which the firm operates and the direction of future trends. An industry analysis should examine the competitive forces from within and outside the industry. Factors will include:

- the demographics of the community served;
- the impact of technology on the delivery of services;
- future efficiencies that will be achieved in the processing of the firm's transactions;
- national trends in the industry;
- global trends in the industry;
- an evaluation of the general economic climate from a short, medium, and long-term perspective;
- the direction of regulatory oversight of the industry.

While many of these analyses are clearly subjective, it is vital to have full hearings on these topics and a synthesis of the perceptions of management as to the environment in which the firm operates.

The SWOT Analysis

The next step is to conduct a SWOT analysis. This requires a totally candid view of the enterprise. Strengths, weaknesses, opportunities, and threats should be assessed by all management employees, with input from the staff. The list of attributes in each case should be as exhaustive as possible, consider present and future market conditions, and include competitive factors related to all providers of financial services.

The Strategic Plan

The last step in this process is to craft a strategic plan. This plan will incorporate the results of the three prior steps to outline:

- overarching goals, and
- specific strategies to achieve these goals.

The time frame covered by the strategic plan should be at least five years with intermediate milestones specified. While goals are general in nature, strategies are more specific.

Using a technology firm as an example, Figure 2.2 shows sample goals and strategies that might accompany them.

Growing Through Merger

Both of the examples of goals and strategies in Figure 2.2 suggest a need for future growth by the firm – the first, growth in overall revenue, the second, growth in corporate software business. If the company's management determines that these strategies cannot reasonably be realized in the context of the current organization, it may be the right time to consider a merger with a firm with attributes that will complement this growth initiative. Likewise, if it appears that containing costs in the current organi-

---

FIGURE 2.2

Sample Goals and Strategies Within a Strategic Plan

Goal 1   **To become one of the most efficient providers of computer services in the region.**

Strategy 1.1   Increase total revenue by 50% within three years and by 100% within five years.

Strategy 1.2   Increase total operating expense by no more than 25% for the next three years and by no more than 50% over the next five years.

Goal 2   **To become one of the strongest marketers of corporate software in the region within five years.**

Strategy 2.1   Within one year, redesign the work flow pattern to facilitate the cross-selling of software products by all representatives with corporate client contact.

Strategy 2.2   Within one year, restructure offerings of corporate software to include a full range of customer accounting, inventory management, and capital budgeting systems.

Strategy 2.3   Within four years, develop a fully integrated system that incorporates every aspect of business within a corporate client environment with systems that share information automatically.

Strategy 2.4   Increase revenue from corporate business to 200% of current revenues within three years and to 500% of current revenues within five years.

---

zation may be difficult while still growing revenues, it may be an appropriate time to consider merging with another similar company to consolidate overhead expense while maintaining an equivalent level of service and revenues.

In essence, the right time to merge will depend on the company's view of its position in the market, its strengths and weaknesses, and its future direction. If there are elements of the strategic plan that may be accomplished best by combining with another enterprise, then it is the right time to merge.

THE RIGHT MERGER PARTNER

2

Within the context of a strategic plan, the right merger partner will offer one or more of the following attributes:

- product diversification
- cost reductions on a per-dollar-of-assets basis
- geographic expansion
- expertise in an area of service that has been targeted through the strategic plan.

FIGURE 2.3

Factors to Consider in Identifying the Right Merger Partner

- Size, History, and Status
- Main Products and Strategies
- Geographic Location and Market Share
- Client/Customer Base
- Operational and Financial Costs
- Quality of Management
- Nature of Ownership
- Legal Status
- Human Resources Profile
- Corporate Culture and Decision-making Process

An analysis of a potential merger partner should consider a number of aspects, including the institution itself, its products and strategies, market position, customers, costs, organization, ownership, legal and environmental considerations, human resource management, and culture (see Figure 2.3). The following lists illustrate the points that should be covered in this analysis.

Lists of Characteristics

Description of the Merger Candidate

- A short history of the development and performance of the potential merger candidate.
- The main lines of business and the location of the candidate's office or store network.
- The size of the candidate firm.
- A description of the balance sheet ratios with respect to the mix of accounts receivable, inventory, and fixed assets; short-term borrowings versus long-term debt, that is, the use of leverage.
- The management of the potential merger candidate, including the extent of experience and the depth of qualified management.
- The candidate's main strengths and weaknesses.
- The candidate's relationships with regulatory agencies.
- Information about previous mergers with other firms and the experiences associated with those mergers.

Main Products and Strategies

- The candidate's product mix, including assets, liabilities, and off-balance sheet categories.
- The history of successful and unsuccessful product development.
- The profitability of the candidate's line of business.
- The perception of the quality of services offered by merger candidate.
- Potential new products being considered.
- Market share of the merger candidate.

Market Position

- Geographic markets served by the candidate.
- Market share controlled by the candidate.
- The candidate's image and reputation within the industry.
- Likely changes in the market position of the merger candidate.

Customers of the Merger Candidate

- The main clientele groups of the candidate.
- The current service needs of the clientele.
- The changing service needs of the clientele.
- The image and reputation of the candidate among its clientele.
- The impact of a merger on the clientele.

Cost Configuration

- The merger candidate's operational efficiency.
- The condition of its operational systems.
- The extent of the use of technology within its operational systems.
- The cost of the candidate's capital.
- Salaries expense as a percentage of the candidate's revenues.

Specific Organization and Management

- The formal organization chart.
- Information about the "informal" organization, including powerful members of the central decision-making team.
- The board of directors.
- Backgrounds and competencies of the key managers.
- Apparent motivation of the key managers in terms of career goals and realized advancement to date.
- Compensation packages of key managers.

Ownership of the Merger Candidate

- Is ownership closely or widely held?
- Who are the shareholders?

- How is control of the candidate exercised?
- What are the shareholder voting arrangements?
- What warrants, rights, and/or stock options are outstanding?
- Which shareholders want to sell their stock?
- Why do these shareholders want to sell?

Legal and Environmental Considerations

- Where is the merger candidate incorporated?
- Where does the stock trade?
- Are there mortgage obligations or other liens that could affect the sale of assets?
- Are there significant unfunded pension and/or medical retirement benefits?
- Are there any active lawsuits involving the candidate?
- Are there any other contracts or informal obligations that should be taken into consideration?
- Are there any environmental issues that affect the operation of the candidate?
- Does the candidate have adequate insurance – both property/casualty and errors/omissions?

Human Resource Management

- What are the strengths and weaknesses of the management team?
- What are the skills and capabilities of the firm's staff?
- Do the employees of the merger candidate appear to be well motivated?
- Do the employees appear to identify with the current owner(s) and management team?
- What is the breakdown of employees and managers by job classification?
- What are the salary levels of these job classifications and are they comparable to the industry?
- What is the age and seniority of the firm's staff and management team?

- What level of education does the staff have?
- What is the extent of employee turnover by job classification and how does it compare with the industry average?
- What provisions exist for overtime work, part-time employees, and temporary employees?
- What are the description and cost of the existing package of fringe benefits, including vacation, health care, profit-sharing, and stock purchase plans?
- How do these provisions compare with those of the company performing the analysis?

2

Corporate Culture

- What is the candidate's management style?
- What is the nature of the "group spirit?"
- Are decisions made centrally or are many decisions made at the work-group level?
- How are the functions of the firm organized – retail versus corporate sales or manufacturing versus service?
- What is the relative power of these functional areas with respect to decision making?
- What is the philosophy of management with respect to: expansion, organizational planning, future industry trends, product development, marketing, financing, and dividend payments to shareholders?
- Are the philosophies of the merger candidate comparable with those of the firm performing the analysis?

These points can be helpful in constructing an objective framework in which to measure the appropriateness of pursuing merger discussions with a potential candidate. The objective is not only to identify an organization with characteristics that are comparable to those of the firm performing the analysis, but also to identify those institutions that have competencies that will complement and facilitate the realization of organizational goals and strategies.

More on Corporate Culture

When companies combine, their staffs almost immediately begin to focus on differences between the companies. One staff may see themselves as winners while the other side is viewed as losers. The controlling company wants to impose changes and may see the other company as highly resistant to change. On the other hand, the other company may feel that the controlling company doesn't "appreciate" them. Then the two sides begin to keep score, tallying which side wins or loses on each issue.

In these situations, it is critical for the perceived "winning" firm to go out of its way to acknowledge as many positive aspects of the acquired firm as possible, and at the same time to create an environment in which there is a high level of openness to change.

It is, in fact, important to identify which cultural factors have historically made an organization so appealing for the combination of the two firms. For example, if a company's historical success was based on its culture of service and quality, rapid and insensitive cost cutting could begin to destroy what made it great.

Likewise, the combination of a small, highly entrepreneurial firm with a larger, more formalized company creates cultural challenges. It is often important to provide direction and additional structure. However, this must be done without killing the entrepreneurial spirit that attracted the larger company in the first place.

One of the difficulties in blending two corporate cultures is that each sees the world through its own cultural filter. This is sometimes referred to as "familiarity blindness" or as a "cultural trance." For example, if everyone in a circle seems averse to risk, then it will appear to the group that the entire world shares this perspective.

COMMUNICATING MERGER BENEFITS

Once managers and directors of two firms have concluded merger negotiations, all other interested parties must then be convinced of the wisdom of the combination. This communication will occur at several levels:

- employee communications
- shareholder communications
- press communications/press releases
- professional market analyst briefings.

The timing of these communications is critical. Employees should be the
first to learn of events, followed shortly by shareholders, and then the
media. It is vital that employees and shareholders do not learn of a
merger from the media. Such a sequence will lead almost certainly to feel-
ings of disenfranchisement and alienation – subsequently leading to difficulties in consolidating the two entities. At the same time, leaking
information about the merger too far in advance will encourage illegal
speculation in the stock market based on insider information.[1]

The key element in this communication is that value will be added to
the institutions involved in the merger. The following information
should be communicated.

- The nature of the agreement, the size of the resulting company, and the
  resulting ranking of the new firm either nationally or regionally.
- The geographic market that the combined organization will service.
- The new name of the organization and its headquarters.
- The officers of the new organization and the composition of the new
  board of directors.

---

[1] Trading in takeover stocks with the expectation of making a profit using undisclosed, market-
sensitive information is referred to in the USA as *misappropriation* of nonpublic information by
the Securities and Exchange Commission and is prohibited by SEC Rule 10b-5. Officers, directors, and other corporate officials owning at least 10 percent of the company's stock must
report trades to the SEC.

- The compensation to shareholders, both stock and cash, as applicable.
- If shareholders have an option of receiving stock or cash, the date by which this election must be made.
- The market value of the merger at current stock prices.
- Whether the merger has any immediate dilutive effects on the stock of either firm.
- The long-term benefits of the merger in terms of shareholders and the market that it serves.
- Any cost reduction plans and how such cost reduction will increase shareholder wealth.
- The anticipated time frame over which the cost reductions will be completed.
- How the two organizations will complement each other in terms of relative strengths and weaknesses.
- How the merger will better position the institution for long-term viability.
- The strategic focus of the new organization.
- Any further approvals that are necessary, such as shareholder approval of both firms and the approval of federal regulatory agencies.
- The date by which any further approvals are expected to be received.
- Stock market listing of the stock of the new company and the anticipated level of dividend payments.
- The investment bankers that have been involved in the merger.
- The opinions of these investment bankers with respect to stock valuation and exchange ratios of the stock of the respective companies.
- Selected pro forma financial information about the individual and merged entities, including: cash and securities, receivables, inventory, fixed assets, liabilities, equity, net income, return on assets, return on equity, debt-to-equity ratios, number of offices or locations, number of cities in which offices are located, number of shareholders, and number of employees.

This information should be contained in any press release provided for general media purposes at the time of the merger announcement.

The communication of the details of the merger is the first critical step in introducing the merger to all concerned parties. However, it must be followed by in-house information sessions with employees, including question and answer sessions. These sessions will help to clarify any questions not directly addressed by the information provided by management. Such sessions play an important role in assuring employees that management is committed to keeping the staff fully apprised of the status and progress of the merger. In other words, the communication of all relevant information is a vital exercise in "full disclosure" to the employees, who must have a sense of trust in the process in order for the new enterprise to realize the anticipated benefits of merging.

In addition, broadcast and print media advertising may be undertaken to convey to customers, first, the culture of the new company, second, the philosophy of the new institution, and, third, the improvement in services that the customers can anticipate. These communications will help ensure customer loyalty and a general attitude of open-mindedness to the change. This is particularly true for a company that will undertake a name change.

An ongoing media campaign for financial market analysts should not be overlooked. Almost all mergers are completed by swapping stock to at least some extent. Most involve the exchange of stock at some predetermined exchange ratio. The value of the stock to be exchanged and, thus, the value of the merger to shareholders, will be based on the perception of the stock market in terms of the wisdom and effectiveness of the merger. The perception of the stock market will be filtered through stock market analysts. The firm's communication with these analysts should be given top priority. Poor communications not only can affect shareholder wealth in the context of a merger currently being undertaken, but can also hurt the prospects for future mergers that will be based on stock swaps. (See Figure 2.4.)

FIGURE 2.4

The Golden Rules of Communicating the Benefits of the Merger

- Communicate to employees, shareholders, the media, and financial market analysts

- Communicate increased value and enhanced service

- Communicate early

- Communicate frequently

- Communicate honestly

- Communicate the resolution of uncertainty

Effective communication of the process and benefits of merging will have many positive effects. Shareholders will be less likely to challenge the merger, employees will be more receptive to change, and market analysts will have reasonable expectations of the future performance of the merged firm.

CONSOLIDATING THE TWO FIRMS

Careful and thoughtful communication of merger plans must be followed by equally well planned implementation of the merger. To be most effective, the implementation plan (at least a blueprint for the implementation plan) should have been drafted prior to merger announcement. If this is not the case, the transition can move very slowly and the strategic and economic value of the merger can be lost, delaying and perhaps reducing the shareholder value effects of combining the two institutions.

The implementation plan should include a transition team that is composed of executives from each institution. Each functional area should also have a specific plan for consolidation with projected completion dates for key elements of the transition. There are a number of important caveats with respect to merger implementation.

- Recognize that a merger consolidation is a rapid, traumatic change that redefines all operations.
- Recognize that the longer the consolidation takes, the more likely it is that customers will be lost, new product offerings will not materialize, key employees will resign, and competing firms will take advantage of what appears to be chaos or, at least, indecisiveness.
- Avoid assembling a transition team that is too large to co-ordinate meeting schedules effectively or make decisions in a timely fashion.
- Make a commitment to keep the lines of communication open during the implementation phase, sharing both realized goals and unanticipated problems.
- Move quickly to resolve the sensitive issues that are most likely to create animosity and derail the consolidation process – salaries, titles, positions, and other issues related to personal opportunity and security.
- Recognize that each management team will have vested interests in maintaining its own procedures or, at a minimum, probably will believe that its procedures are "best practice."
- Be prepared to redesign procedures to achieve the best results for the new organization.

In a merger of equals, the two institutions are presumed to have equivalent power to make decisions within the consolidated entity. Expectations of such even-handed control can be frustrated, however, unless both parties in the merger recognize that their autonomy will be constrained by the compromises which necessarily accompany any business combination.

Decisions Concerning Practices and Procedures

In evaluating the practices that will be adopted by the combined firm, the transition team should be prepared to examine each functional area objectively. This process should be geared to creating efficiencies in operating expense while still maintaining high-quality service.

In every case, quality control should be stressed. The most efficient operation will spend the least amount of time correcting errors. Time spent undoing tasks that have been improperly executed is time wasted and can lead to actual losses to the firm.

Operational Systems

Systems integration can take place after the "best practice" approach has been identified in each area. There is no single best approach to this integration process. However, generally, there are three ways that systems integration can be accomplished:

- one firm can adopt totally the systems of the other (absorption);
- the two firms can maintain separate systems;
- the two firms can mix the best of both systems, for example, using the receivables system of one and the payables system of the other (best practices).

Absorption

The circumstance under which one company would adopt the systems of the other is more often appropriate in the case of the combination of a large company with a considerably smaller firm. Such a combination is more often characterized as an acquisition rather than a merger. The "absorption" of one system by another is fast and generates the greatest savings among the three alternatives. The greatest economies of scale are possible through extensive consolidation of back office systems. The operation of only one of the two firms is affected and the actual cost of conversion is minimized. However, this approach can create dissension among the managers of the entity doing the conversion and the "identity" of the converting firm may be lost.

Separate Systems

Maintaining separate systems may be the correct alternative if the two companies are in different and distant locations. Clearly, modifying systems can be time-consuming and expensive. Maintaining separate systems encourages autonomous operation, helps preserve the identity of both firms, and avoids the necessity to (and the cost of) terminating existing systems' contracts. However, the degree of long-term cost savings associated with maintaining separate systems is limited. There are no economies of scale, back-office consolidation is not possible, and the companies appear to be two different entities.

Best Practices

The third alternative of selecting among the systems for the "best practice" system in each area takes considerably more time and can become a political process if each management team fights to maintain its systems. This alternative is also more expensive than the other two alternatives because the systems of both companies changes. However, this approach emphasizes the equality of the partners in the merger, allows the partners to appear as one entity to its customers, and results in the best possible systems.

In some cases, the systems of one of the two firms may be in considerable need of modernization. Such an example might be a holding company that has five different inventory and customer accounting systems with software applications that have not been updated for over ten years. Obviously, correcting such deficiencies can be expensive. Accordingly, it is extremely important that the review of operational systems be initiated immediately upon commencement of merger talks.[2]

Building Working Relationships

At the heart of consolidation of the two companies is the ability to communicate among the transition team, management teams, and staffs. In

---

[2] See the discussion of cost configuration in the section above entitled "The Right Merger Partner."

turn, the ability to communicate depends to a large extent on the perceptions of these individuals and their shared perceptions. While managers may feel that managing perceptions is less significant than the other pressing issues surrounding a merger, these tendencies must be resisted. Subtle, but important, actions can vastly improve the comfort level and effectiveness of working relationships.

Immediately after a merger, recruiters often attempt to hire away the best and brightest managers and technical personnel to competing firms with attractive financial incentives. To minimize this activity, the new combined firm may offer sign-up bonuses – so-called "stay bonuses" – to persuade key managers to remain with the firm. These bonuses may include stock options, stock grants, and long or short-term cash incentives.

In this process, however, management should not lose sight of the objective – to keep the best people and to keep these people motivated. The incentives should be linked to the creation of economic value for the firm. One popular technique creates an incentive "pool" that consists of a percentage of the new value created by the merged management team.

Sound compensation planning can be the catalyst to break post-merger inertia and allow organizations to capture the values that drove and justified the transaction. The planning, designing, implementing, and communicating of compensation programs address the most important link between employee and employer. When these compensation issues are addressed quickly and effectively, the negative effects of a prolonged transition are minimized.

The greater the differences in compensation philosophy, the greater the risk and difficulty in combining compensation plans. How can philosophies of pay and benefits be compared? One good way to assess differences in compensation plans is the "risk-to-reward" ratio. At one extreme is the security-oriented organization that generally pays only fixed salaries and offers defined benefits. At the other end of the spectrum are companies whose plans are highly leveraged with significant amounts of compensation at risk under various incentive arrangements. The new combined entity should rest comfortably on the appropriate spot along this continuum.

Whatever compensation system is chosen, managers can build credibility by perceived truthfulness of communication, demonstration of personal competence and fairness, and delivery of resources to accomplish the specified target outcomes. The early statements with respect to the merger and its effects must be perceived as true and followed by appropriate actions. When managers provide real assistance in the transition process and perform as promised, the trust of the firm's staff and other members of the management team is strengthened. This trust helps to increase the likelihood that the best employees will be encouraged to stay and perform. Most importantly, low morale will not hamper the progress of the merger.

THE DECISION TO SELL THE COMPANY

In some cases, a review of the strengths and weaknesses of a firm leads its directors to the conclusion that the best way to maximize the value of shareholder wealth is for the company to be merged with another company. This may be at least partially attributable to relative illiquidity of the company's stock.

Generally, healthy companies can expect to be approached about the prospect of selling the firm. In many cases, the company being approached has little experience with mergers. (In some cases, the company that suggests merger discussions also has little experience.) It is better to consider this issue *before* being approached to avoid making ill-advised decisions. Should the company sell or remain independent? The answer to this question should be driven by the same process that supports the decision to seek merger partners: an established mission, an objective assessment of the firm in the context of industry trends, and a strategic plan.

However, once an unsolicited bid has been received, the company's directors first must decide whether to respond to the offer. If there is no genuine interest to pursue a merger, generally no response is required.[3] However, if there is genuine interest (as opposed to simple curiosity), the directors of the target firm must consider several factors:

- the origin and impact of the offer
- the process of evaluating the offer
- the attractiveness of the offer.

The Origin and Impact of the Offer

Questions with respect to the origin and impact of the offer center around the bidder and the consequences of selling under the terms of the offer. Does the bidder have substantial business background and a long-term strategic plan that is consistent with the current offer? These considerations speak to the issues of whether the shareholders initially will perceive the offer as a serious one and, likewise, whether the bidder has serious intentions.

Also, has the bidder provided evidence that the deal can be financed if cash or debt is to be used? What impact would this financing have on the company? A highly leveraged transaction will have more wealth shifting characteristics than a more straightforward equity exchange. In a leveraged financing, the shareholders of the bidder may realize a substantial profit by using debt financing to acquire control of the target firm and selling the firm's assets to repay some portion of the debt, gaining control with relatively little investment. In the meantime, the firm's current shareholders may be forced to exchange equity for riskier debt securities with uncertain market characteristics and little or no potential for capital appreciation.

---

[3] If there is no interest and the directors respond, they risk unnecessarily encouraging the bidder, eliciting a stronger offer from the bidder, market rumors that lead to speculation in the stock, and needlessly raising concerns by shareholders and employees about the future of the firm.

Also important are the plans of the bidder relative to treatment of employees and management of the firm. Will some or all of the employees be retained? What will be the roles and designations of the managers? Will the board of directors continue to exist after the merger? What will be the new corporate name of the entity?

Evaluating the Offer

2

With respect to evaluating the offer, there are several basic issues to be addressed to ensure sound decision making and to avoid subsequent legal actions against the board of directors by shareholders dissatisfied with decisions of the board.

- What written information has the board received concerning the offer? To begin the evaluation process, the directors must have complete, reliable information about the offer itself.
- How much time does the board have to respond? A timetable for evaluating the offer must give the directors adequate time to, first, individually consider the offer and, second, collectively discuss the issues to arrive at a decision or counteroffer.
- Does the board understand its legal obligations? The directors should have a written legal opinion as to their duties from experienced, independent counsel. This opinion should include a description of all laws that apply to directors in the home country or state of the merged firm.
- What support do the directors have in the evaluation process? The board should have the input of consultants, investment bankers, attorneys, and accountants. In this way, the directors will be able to assess the implications of the merger from all relevant perspectives – operational, financial, legal, and accounting.
- Does management of the firm have the technical expertise to evaluate and negotiate the offer? Since a merger has major implications in terms of all aspects of the firm, management must also be able to provide input to the decision-making process. A negotiation team should have

39

representation from all functional areas of the firm and have clearly defined duties, goals, and strategies.

■ Has the process of documenting the decision-making process been determined? It is not sufficient to conduct a well planned, comprehensive review of the merger offer. The board of directors must be able to demonstrate and document that this process has occurred. This documentation must provide evidence of the board's caution, diligence, and competence.

Attractiveness of the Offer

In terms of the attractiveness of the offer, the board must consider the structure of the deal. Are the financial terms generally attractive? Is the deal legal and feasible? Will the merger have a positive total effect on the company and its shareholders?

If the answer to one or more of these questions is "no," the board has the obligation to identify alternatives for purposes of a counteroffer. Also, the board must consider the legal status of the bidder in terms of lawsuits or regulatory problems that could prevent the bidder from completing the merger as specified.

The consideration of these issues places substantial responsibility on the board of directors. These responsibilities may also be affected by other regulatory requirements. For example, some jurisdictions permit corporations to include in their articles of incorporation a requirement that directors consider the interests of parties other than stock holders in mergers and acquisitions.

A PROFOUND DECISION

The decision to merge or to be merged has implications far beyond the price paid. It is not a decision made in isolation, nor should the decision be made in haste. Once the decision to merge is made, the right merger partner is the key to success. Proper planning, open communications, and decisive action after the merger announcement will ensure the success of the combined entity.

Selected References

Ernst & Young (1994) *Mergers and Acquisitions*. 2nd edn. New York: John Wiley & Sons.

Haspeslagh, Jemison, D. B. and Philippe C. (1991) *Managing Acquisitions: Creating Value Through Corporate Renewal*. New York: The Free Press.

Rock, M. L., Rock, R. H., and Sikora, M. (1994) *The Mergers & Acquisitions Handbook*. 2nd edn. New York: McGraw-Hill.

2

CHAPTER 3

ACQUISITIONS

Introduction

◼

Acquisition Guidelines

◼

The Acquisition Agreement

◼

Using Brokers and Finders

◼

Defending Against Acquisitions

◼

Managing the Transition

◼

The Art of the Deal

◼

Addendum 3.1: Hostile Takeovers in Europe

INTRODUCTION

A merger is called an *acquisition* when one of the firms in the transaction, usually the larger, takes over the other company and consolidates the two organizations into a single entity. The acquirer's name is usually retained and control of the decision-making process rests almost entirely with the acquirer. Acquisitions facilitate growth into new geographic areas and new product lines. A successful acquisition program must be carefully structured to analyze potential acquisition candidates, consider all the appropriate factors, and reach an equitable acquisition agreement.

3

ACQUISITION GUIDELINES

The process of increasing market share through acquisitions should begin with the same process that drives corporate mergers. A well conceived strategic plan will serve as guidance in terms of correct timing and identifying the appropriate acquisition target(s). (See Chapter 2, sections entitled "The Right Time to Merge" and "The Right Merger Partner.") In addition, a successful acquisition program involves:

- assembling the right acquisition team;
- narrowing the field of acquisition targets;
- designing strategies to approach the acquisition target;
- structuring an effective acquisition agreement;
- deciding on the use of brokers and finders.

The Acquisition Team

The managers and outside consultants that are members of the acquisition team will reflect the competencies that are required to effectively negotiate with and integrate the acquisition target. The team should include legal experts, accountants or lawyers that are familiar with tax law, finance professionals, and investment bankers.

Legal Experts

The legal experts will provide important input concerning the takeover of a public corporation. These members of the team will be responsible for the review of applicable state and federal securities laws, the antitrust considerations (market concentration, for example), necessary regulatory approvals, and the legal implications of alternative acquisition strategies. If the acquisition target is not a publicly traded corporation, internal counsel of the acquiring company may be able to provide guidance in the legal issues involved in the acquisition. Even if the internal legal staff is competent in the matters involved with the acquisition, retaining outside counsel can enhance the effectiveness and speed with which the acquisition is completed.

Tax Experts

The involvement of accountants or lawyers that are familiar with tax law is necessary in order to structure the most tax-effective deal. The tax specialists should review the various tax structures that are available for the acquisition and run scenario analyses based on relevant tax considerations. In this way, the team can identify the best alternative from a tax perspective. The scenario analyses should consider the impact of the acquisition on all classes of shareholders – individual, corporate, and trust. Even if the most efficient tax structure is not possible, the analysis can measure the opportunity cost of the tax structure that is adopted. Also, the tax members of the team can determine whether it is necessary to obtain a tax authority ruling. If the seller requires a tax ruling, the time frame of the transaction must accommodate this process.

Finance Professionals

Finance professionals must be involved at the early stages of the acquisition analysis to provide input with respect to the value of the acquisition target and the economic impact of the combination. Relevant issues include, first, whether the transaction should be cash versus a stock swap and, second, whether special provisions are necessary to address the value of stock to be exchanged (for example, provisions in the event of significant declines in market value of the acquirer's stock). The finance professionals should also evaluate the impact of purchase versus pooling accounting for the transaction.

The finance professionals should evaluate the composition of the acquiree's balance sheet, including:

■ level of inventories
■ age of accounts receivable
■ leverage (debt) effects
■ capital equipment composition
■ off-balance-sheet exposures such as derivative transactions or contingent liabilities.

The effect of income synergies should also be considered – cross-selling opportunities, overhead efficiencies, and other relevant income considerations.

In essence, the finance professionals give the most comprehensive view of the new combined institution after the transaction is complete.

Investment Bankers

Investment bankers are essential for transactions of all sizes if the acquisition target is a public firm. An investment banker should also be part of the team if the transaction involves a larger firm that is privately held. In selecting an investment banking firm, the employees of the acquiring enterprise (that are a part of the acquisition team) should meet with the representative(s) of the investment bank to assess the ability of the firm to handle the transaction and the representatives' familiarity with similar transactions. Once an investment banking firm is selected, the acquiring company should document the selection in a formal engagement letter. These professionals should be involved in all aspects of the acquisition – providing advice on acquisition strategies, high-level access to target management, fairness opinions with respect to valuation, deal structuring (cash and/or stock, timing of offer, etc.), financial advice, and tactics during implementation of the acquisition.

Narrowing the Field of Acquisition Targets

A Preliminary List

Guidelines for identifying potential acquisition targets should be based on the strategic plan for the acquiring company. Given the large number of firms in most industries, the identification process should involve all members of the acquisition team. When assembling a preliminary list of potential target firms, the team should bear in mind the availability of potential targets. The probability of a successful acquisition will be increased if the company in question:

- has been a recent takeover target in a deal that was not completed (this demonstrates serious consideration of a sale of the firm);
- is the subject of takeover rumors (this suggests that the firm is at least discussing the possibility);
- has undergone recent substantial top management changes (appears to be ready for a significant change in corporate governance);
- appears to be receptive to acquisition for other reasons.

The sources of possible candidates include the internal and external members of the acquisition team, the financial or business press, market analysts, and business and personal acquaintances. Of course, if the acquiring firm has a specific geographic market in mind, the preliminary list could include all companies in that geographic region.

A Parameter Search

If the acquiring firm has access to a database of companies in the industry, the preliminary list of acquisition candidates can include those identified through a parameter search. A parameter search involves constructing a model of the institution that is sought using variables that describe location, size, profitability, asset mix, industry mix, and other key factors. For example, using the first parameter, the database is searched for those firms that satisfy the location parameters. The list of resulting firms is then reduced to those that satisfy the size parameters. This process continues until all parameters have been introduced.

Review of Publicly Available Information

Once the preliminary list of potential acquisition candidates has been created, the next step is to conduct a full review of the candidates on the list with publicly available information. This review includes:

- apparent availability for acquisition
- financial analysis
- market share
- client base
- market dynamics
- hidden assets (for example, critical patents or other proprietary assets)
- hidden liabilities (for example, unfunded pension plans)
- any significant regulatory issues (that potentially could block the acquisition).

Qualitative Issues

If a particular candidate passes through these filters, the next step is to consider qualitative issues, that is, more subjective, motivational issues with respect to the target firm.

- Do the owners want to sell?
- Is there an apparent problem with management succession?
- Have the directors of the company strongly disagreed on important issues?
- How much stock do the managers own?
- Have the managers and directors been selling or buying stock?

The answers to these questions will help the acquisition team to structure a deal that has the highest probability of acceptance.

Approaching the Acquisition Target

In general there are three ways an acquiring firm can approach a target firm:

- friendly persuasion approach
- opportunistic approach
- completely unnegotiated approach.

Friendly Persuasion Approach

The friendly persuasion approach is one in which the acquiring firm attempts to convince the target to negotiate its sale. The advantages of this approach are that it is likely to be the least expensive in terms of time and legal cost, management of the target firm is more likely to remain with the firm, and the acquiring firm will have access to more and better information about the target firm. The acquiring firm will succeed with this approach to the extent that:

- directors and managers do not have a strong propensity to remain independent;
- the chief executive of the acquiring company has or can establish good rapport with the chief executive of the acquisition candidate;
- the price that is being offered appears attractive.

In the friendly persuasion approach, it should be remembered that the chief executive of the target firm probably has little incentive to sell because a sale will undoubtedly dilute his or her power. Also, the chief executive will be vitally concerned about the confidentiality of the discussions, lest rumors drive market dynamics to force a sale of the firm. That is, rumors will force up the market value of the stock. If a sale of the firm does not materialize, the stock price is likely to plummet – causing considerable concern on the part of shareholders and an uncomfortable situation for the chief executive.

Opportunistic Approach

Opportunistic approaches take advantage of a situation in which the acquisition target

- has already been targeted by another, unfriendly firm that is attempting an acquisition;
- has communicated its availability for sale through a broad solicitation being managed by an intermediary (often an investment bank); or
- has agreed to be sold to another firm.

3

If the acquisition target is subject to a hostile takeover from a third firm, the acquiring firm can act as a "white knight," that is, a friendly potential buyer, by communicating early on its interest in initiating acquisition discussions. Even if the takeover attempt has progressed into a full-fledged battle with the third firm, it may be possible for the acquiring firm to enter as a "grey knight" (not altogether friendly), with an attractive offer before a deal is finalized.

In the second case – in which the targeted firm has announced its availability for sale – it is possible to convert this solicitation into a friendly persuasion approach by preempting the auction phase and transforming the process into a one-to-one negotiation. Given time constraints, however, the acquiring firm must be extremely responsive to the seller's price and nonprice objectives and be willing to work virtually around the clock, retain competent advisers to work on the offer, and perform whatever tasks are necessary to complete the deal.

Under the third condition – in which a firm has agreed to be acquired by a third company – the transaction is called a "swipe." The acquiring company offers a higher price than that already accepted by the board of directors. The swipe is most often employed when the third party is a group of managers, that is, the case of a management-led buy-out. In such cases, outside directors may have felt the pressure of potential conflicts of interest associated with an insider acquisition and perhaps even felt that the insider offer was associated with a price that was too low.

Completely Unnegotiated Approach

Completely unnegotiated approaches are most often associated with the 1980s. This approach is any unilateral attempt by an acquiring firm to gain control of an acquisition target without the approval of the firm's management or board of directors, that is, a hostile takeover. In many cases, this type of approach followed the "nibbler" strategy in which the acquiring firm bought from just under 5 percent of the stock of the acquisition target to 25 percent or more. It should be noted that in most countries any purchase of stock of a public company in excess of a stated percentage, perhaps 5 percent, must be accompanied by registration with that country's securities authorities. Generally, the registration involves disclosure of the amount of stock purchased and purchaser's intentions with respect to the company. Typically, when the nibbler strategy has been employed, the acquiring firm buys a stake and then makes a tender offer for the rest of the stock.

Often the acquiring firm is in an ideal position to profit. Either enough stock is purchased without paying a premium to substantially lower the effective cost of the acquisition, or the acquiring firm subsequently sells the partial stake at a substantial premium back to the target firm or to a "white knight" bidder.

In the USA, the completely unnegotiated approach has been used less frequently in recent years for a number of reasons:

- some states have enacted laws to guard against such actions;
- stock market volatility has caused outcomes to be far less predictable;
- it is much more difficult to get financing from banks, insurance companies, and the junk bond market for these transactions.

(See also Addendum 3.1 at the end of this chapter for a discussion of hostile takeovers in Europe.)

THE ACQUISITION AGREEMENT

Negotiating an agreement for an acquisition is usually a long and complicated task. The parties involved must cooperate to ensure the best interests of the firm are served. The acquisition agreement is the formal, legal version of the sum of all discussions among the parties. It is the articulation of the often oversimplified ideas of the parties as to the terms of the transaction.

3

A large number of issues must be addressed. The agreement is intended to answer – in advance – questions that might otherwise lead to confusion, differing interpretations, dispute, and, ultimately, litigation. In its purest form, it accurately and unambiguously sets forth all the rights and obligations of the parties to the agreement.

The agreement should include:

- representations and warranties
- covenants
- conditions necessary to close the deal
- indemnification.

Representations and warranties provide information to the acquiring firm, protect the acquirer in the event that unanticipated adverse facts are discovered, and form the framework of the position of the selling firm. Seller's representations and warranties usually compose the largest part of the acquisition agreement.

Covenants are usually negative and prevent the acquired firm from taking certain actions without the consent of the acquiring firm. Examples might be to *not* change accounting procedures or enter into additional long-term contracts. Other, positive, covenants obligate one or both parties in the transaction to take certain actions prior to closing. Examples of positive covenants might be the seller allowing the purchaser full access to books of account and other records and filing the appropriate documents with government authorities charged with overseeing business combinations.

In general, conditions necessary to close are straightforward requirements. Examples include receiving approval by regulatory authorities, receiving financial statements, settling litigation, and signing key personnel to employment agreements.

Indemnification covers the period of time after the acquisition is closed or the transaction is complete. Indemnification covers inaccurate or incomplete representations and warranties, liability to third parties, and other material aspects of the acquisition. These clauses can protect either the acquired or the acquiring firm.

The First Step: Agreement in Principle

While the acquisition agreement represents the culmination of acquisition, the start of negotiations is marked by an agreement in principle, often called a letter of intent or memorandum of understanding. A letter of intent may set forth little more than a sketch of the principal points of agreement. Nevertheless, it can serve useful purposes.

- Although generally not legally binding, the letter of intent creates a moral obligation that generally is a serious obligation of both sides.
- The letter of intent outlines the basic terms of the transaction, reducing the likelihood of subsequent misunderstandings.

It should be noted that there might be good reasons not to have a letter of intent.

- The parties may not wish to make the public announcement that is generally required of public companies.
- The acquired firm may have been negotiating with other parties and may want to avoid alienating them.
- If important points remain open, a letter of intent may weaken one party's bargaining position.
- Much energy can be wasted in negotiating an agreement in principle that might be better spent in negotiating the definitive agreement.

The form of the agreement in principle is generally a letter from the acquiring firm addressed to the acquired firm or to the shareholders of the acquired firm. It is signed by the purchaser, and countersigned by the seller or the stock holders. Although the agreement in principle is not intended to be legally binding, portions of the letter, such as a confidentiality agreement, may be binding.

A letter of intent should cover the following areas.

3

- A description of the form of transaction-merger, stock purchase, or asset purchase, if known at the time of signing.
- Details of consideration for the purchase. If stock is to be exchanged, the stock exchange ratio or other method of valuation should be explained. If other securities are to be used, these securities should be explained. Any contingent or deferred payments also should be disclosed clearly.
- Protective provisions, such as an escrow or pledge. Escrow provisions are often used when there is a possibility that the target company's future earnings may not meet certain expectations or that potential liability could arise at some time following the closing. Thus, a portion of the purchase price may be set aside for a specified period of time in an escrow account.[1]
- Special arrangements, such as employment contracts with the directors, officers, or employees of the acquired firm.
- Brokers' and finders' fees.
- Any restrictions on the seller's business operations pending the closing.
- A "no-shop" clause that commits the acquired firm neither to solicit other offers nor to provide information to or negotiate with other interested parties.

---

[1] If breaches of representations or warranties are discovered after the closing, all or a portion of the escrow funds are returned to the acquiring firm with the balance paid to the acquired firm. If the acquiring firm issues a promissory note as part of the consideration, the acquired firm may want all or a portion of the assets or stocks acquired by the acquiring firm to be pledged as security for the note's payment.

- A "bust-up" fee to be paid to the acquiring firm if the acquired firm is bought by a third party.

Also, the agreement in principle should include the significant conditions to consummate the transaction, such as:

- execution of a definitive agreement containing representations, warranties, covenants, conditions, and appropriate indemnifications and
- any other conditions that have been discussed, such as tax rulings, financial performance, off-balance-sheet conditions, or agreement on the part of third parties.

Structuring the Acquisition Agreement

The nature of the acquisition will dictate the structure of an acquisition agreement. For example, if the transaction is an acquisition of assets only, the agreement should specify, as clearly as possible, the assets and liabilities that are being transferred. If the entire firm is being sold, that is, the stock of the firm, the consideration for the stock should be clearly outlined.

Generally, acquisition agreements are similar in structure and share a number of principal features, as follows.

- The operative terms of the transaction, including identification of the assets or stock to be acquired, the consideration to be paid, and the mechanics of the transaction.
- Other related terms of the principal transaction, such as earn-out or financing provisions. An earn-out provision is a provision that requires the acquiring firm to make an additional payment(s) if certain contingencies are met, such as the acquired business's attaining specified levels of earnings. A financing provision is one that makes clear that the acquiring firm's ability to pay for the acquired business is subject to its ability to obtain financing from a third party; it also defines the parameters of such financing:
  - the acquired firm's representations and warranties;

– the acquiring firm's representations and warranties;
– the acquired firm's covenants pending closing;
– the acquiring firm's covenants pending the closing;
– conditions to be met by the acquired firm in order to close;
– closing and termination provisions;
– indemnification provisions;
– miscellaneous matters, such as finders' fees, expenses, and particular laws governing the transaction.

3

USING BROKERS AND FINDERS

In the early stages of the acquisition process, it may be necessary to employ the services of an intermediary other than an investment banker. This is especially true if the acquiring company (or a company seeking to be acquired) is a small or medium-sized firm. A broker studies the firm and its objectives, prepares a description of the desired transaction, helps the firm to determine the best strategy to follow in finding an acquisition target (or an acquiring company), and assists in negotiating the terms of the transaction. A finder serves only to introduce the two companies. There are varying degrees of services that can be offered between these two extremes.

Typically, neither brokers nor finders are required by state law to be licensed. However, if the transfer of real estate is involved, the rules concerning real estate brokerage may apply. If the transaction involves the sale of stock instead of assets, federal securities laws in some countries require that a broker be a registered securities dealer.

The right intermediary can be of great assistance in a number of areas. A broker can analyze the structure of each company and suggest an appropriate approach to the acquisition target. A broker also can aid negotiation by acting as a buffer to encourage more open discussions than may otherwise be possible between the acquiring firm and the acquisition target.

The relationship between the firm and the intermediary will depend on the size of the company. If the firm is small, there may be a single-transaction arrangement to find a suitable acquisition or a suitable acquiring company. In either case, the selling enterprise generally pays the intermediary's fee. If the firm is larger, the acquisition team or the merger and acquisition department will have staff with the primary responsibilities of an intermediary. Alternatively, a larger enterprise may use the services of a broker or finder, keeping the intermediary on a retainer.

The fee of an intermediary is contingent on the completion of the transaction and represents some percentage of the value of the transaction. The fee is most often based on the Lehman formula or the "5-4-3-2-1 formula." That is:

- 5 percent is paid on the first $1 million of the transaction
- 4 percent on the amount from $1 million to $2 million
- 3 percent on the amount from $2 million to $3 million
- 2 percent on the amount from $3 million to $4 million
- 1 percent on any amount in excess of $4 million.

However, in small transactions, the intermediary's fee can range between 5 percent and 10 percent of the amount of the transaction. Also, a fixed percentage, instead of a declining scale, may be used in transactions of all sizes. In the event that the broker has special knowledge and expertise about the industry, a premium above the Lehman fee may be assessed. Thus, the fee will depend not only on the amount of the transaction, but also on the services rendered and the expertise of the intermediary.

If a broker performs services beyond simply finding an eventual buyer or seller, a purely contingent fee may be inappropriate. This will be particularly true if the intermediary is retained to find an appropriate acquisition target. In this case, the broker may require payment based on time spent in the search and analysis, perhaps with a retainer against which time is charged, and a contingent fee based on the amount of a completed transaction. There may even be incentive clauses in the agreement. Such clauses are most common in the case of a firm seeking to be acquired. A fixed percentage may be paid up to a specified transaction amount with a higher percentage for amounts above the specified level.

The arrangement between the company and the intermediary should be documented in a written agreement. The specifics of this agreement should include the following.

- The exact parties to the transaction.
- Whether the intermediary is retained on an exclusive or nonexclusive basis. (The agreement is typically nonexclusive, giving a company the right to deal with other firms not introduced through the intermediary.)
- A statement that the broker will assist in negotiations if requested by the contracting firm.
- The definition of a completed transaction. (This can be either all assets, all shares, or some fraction thereof.)
- The fee structure of the arrangement.
- The method by which the proceeds of a completed sale are to be valued. (For example, securities exchanged will be valued based on prices stipulated in the definitive agreement to complete the transaction.)
- A commitment not to disclose any information identified for nondisclosure by the directors or management of the contracting firm.
- The terms under which the arrangement may be terminated.

The most important element in securing the services of a broker or finder is to find an intermediary whose judgment can be trusted. In this way, the contracting firm can avail itself confidently of services that otherwise may not be available to it.

DEFENDING AGAINST ACQUISITIONS

The issue of unsolicited and unwanted bids is addressed by methods used to defend against such overtures. In some cases, the buy-out of executives employed by the acquisition target is made too expensive through "golden parachutes." In other cases, defenses of many varieties, including "poison pills," are used to discourage unwanted solicitations. In all cases, these measures must be kept in perspective. The goal of directors and management always should be to maximize shareholder wealth, which maximization sometimes is associated with an acquisition. Defenses should not conflict with this objective. The correct balance in this trade-off is sometimes difficult to achieve.

The Use of Golden Parachutes

Golden parachutes are compensation packages that cushion the effect of unemployment for an employee after control of the firm has changed hands. Essentially, the employee is offered special payments for leaving the firm if the employee's position is eliminated as a result of the acquisition. From the perspective of the acquisition target, a golden parachute should help reduce resistance to the acquisition as a result of the employee's concern for self-interests. With fewer concerns about personal security, the employee will negotiate in the best interests of the shareholders, who will, in turn, receive the highest price for their stock.

However, the extensive use of these arrangements during the early 1980s drew criticism from institutional investors and regulators. Huge payouts seem to fly in the face of the objective of financial management – to maximize shareholder wealth. The debate about golden parachutes is part of a debate surrounding executive compensation. The main thesis is that executives should be compensated for creating shareholder wealth. To the extent that golden parachutes reward executives that perform so poorly that their companies require a bailout, the associated compensation cannot be justified. For this reason, golden parachutes have become more associated with defenses against unwanted acquisition overtures.

Parachute arrangements can be observed at three different levels:

■ the golden parachute is offered to top executives;
■ the silver parachute is designed for middle managers and their peers;

- the tin parachute covers lower-level employees.

The payment formulas differ depending on the version of the parachute being employed.

The parachute is activated through triggers. A single-trigger releases the parachute if there is a change in control of the firm. This could involve as little as a 20 percent purchase of stock by an acquiring firm and, thus, allows the executive to leave with little real provocation. A double-trigger involves, first, a change in control of the firm which begins a probationary period. The second trigger is pulled if the employee is terminated after the probationary period.

The efforts of institutional investors and regulators to eliminate excessive payouts under golden parachutes and other compensation plans culminated in specific provisions of the Deficit Reduction Act of 1984 in the USA. Any severance package that exceeds three times an executive's average compensation for the five years prior to a change in control lost its tax deduction for the company and created a 20 percent excise tax for the departing executive. The permissible multiple was set at 2.99 times the five-year base by the Internal Revenue Service. Amendments to the Act in 1989 refined some of the concepts of the original Act:

- the composition of the base amount;
- the types of employees that would be considered highly paid and eligible for golden parachutes;
- a one-year period of time that must elapse between the effective date of the golden parachute and the date of change of control.

It should be emphasized that, in the USA, the golden parachute can no longer be used to block an acquisition while it is underway. Also, as all executive compensation comes under closer scrutiny by the US Securities and Exchange Commission, the golden parachute will be subject to increasing disclosure.

Generally speaking, the golden parachute should be considered as part of a total compensation package for an executive, not as simply a mechanism for future defense against acquisition. The compensation committee of the board of directors should evaluate appropriateness, cost/ benefit relationships, and acceptability to shareholders when establishing base compensation and the golden parachute.

Other Acquisition Defenses

Poison pills are rights distributed to shareholders that allow them to buy additional shares under certain defined circumstances and can be used to discourage unwanted solicitations. Many are referred to as shareholder rights plans or shareholder protection plans. There is no evidence of the effectiveness of these measures. Indeed, it appears unlikely that even one announced acquisition has been frustrated solely by defensive mechanisms against acquisition. However, it is entirely possible that acquisitions that were still in the conceptual stage have not been pursued because of apparent obstacles to their completion.

Poison pills take a number of forms.

- The "flip-in" right permits shareholders to buy additional stock at a price far above prevailing market levels. However, should the company be threatened with an unwanted acquisition, the price of additional stock becomes much more attractive. For example, if a tender offer is presented for 30 percent of the shares, existing shareholders can buy more stock at the rate of two shares for the prevailing market price of one share. (The level of stock ownership by the acquiring firm at which the provision becomes effective is referred to as the kick-in threshold.) The objective is to increase the number of shares outstanding and, presumably, the total cost of the acquisition.

- A "flip-over" pill is a second line of defense. If the acquirer is successful in gaining control, the original shareholders have the right to buy shares of the acquiring firm at prices much lower than the prevailing market price. The objective is to demonstrate the potential dilution of the acquirer's stock.

- A "back-end" pill increases the leverage of the firm when the kick-in threshold is reached. Debt securities are issued to shareholders, thereby increasing the liabilities that must be paid by the acquiring firm.

Poison pills have generally survived the court battles over their legality and are not frequently rescinded when institutional investors challenge them in the context of corporate governance.

While poison pills are essentially shareholder provisions, poison securities are issued with provisions that accomplish similar outcomes.

3

- "Poison shares" have normal voting rights in most circumstances but receive much more voting power in the event of an unwanted solicitation or attack. For example, preferred shares may be nonvoting or have one vote per share. When the company is attacked, each preferred shareholder may have ten votes.
- "Poison puts" are attached to debt securities – bonds, notes, and other debt instruments. When an attack is launched or control changes hands, the debt securities become immediately callable and must be redeemed.

Financial engineering may also be used to ward off unwanted bids for the firm.

- A "self-tender" is the large scale repurchase of shares in response to unsolicited bids. This channels cash to shareholders who accept the offers, generally priced above market price, and reduces the number of shares outstanding, usually pushing up the stock price. If borrowed funds are used to purchase the shares, this approach also increases the leverage of the company. The net effect is that the shares become more expensive while the level of debt may also increase.
- An "in-house ESOP" or employee stock ownership plan can hold a substantial percentage of the outstanding stock. The premise of this approach is that the employees will vote against a hostile bid to buy the company.
- "Pension parachutes" are designed to discourage unsolicited bids that are at least partially motivated by overfunded pension plans. During

the 1980s, many acquisition targets were attractive because over-funded pension plans could be terminated and the surplus funding captured, as long as employees in the plan were given an adequate sub-stitute for the terminated plan. The pension parachute removed the economic incentive for this tactic. One type of provision prevents the acquiring firm from gaining access to the pension fund. Another im-mediately increases benefits to retired and existing employees if control of the firm changes hands.

All of these defenses should be considered by any enterprise that has a strong inclination to remain independent. They may, in fact, be appro-priate for a closely held company with shareholders closely involved in management. However, if the ownership is widely held and, particularly, if shareholders include institutional investors, management should be wary of instituting policies that can be interpreted as preventing transac-tions that would enhance shareholder wealth.

MANAGING THE TRANSITION

Perhaps even more than a merger, an acquisition can lead to potentially devastating impacts on productivity of the acquired company and, accordingly, shareholder value. However, the basics of managing the transition are similar with respect to communications and consolidation of the two entities. Special effort should be exerted to guard against the disintegration of morale within the acquired firm.

- Communicate the impending change as soon as negotiations will permit.
- Share the strategic plan with the employees of the acquired company as soon as possible.
- Be prepared to be flexible and creative with necessary job changes, softening the adverse effects for employees as much as possible.
- Invest in the development and retraining of those employees who remain.

The communications process should include meetings with employees, factual press releases, and accurate communication with the market served. This may be more difficult for the management of the acquired firm to accomplish than in the case of a merger. Top management, when faced with an acquisition, may tend to withdraw from the public forum and confer behind closed doors with investment bankers and attorneys, leaving rumors to develop and spread unchecked. Communication to employees who will lose their positions should be accomplished as quickly as possible, with an explanation of why their jobs have been eliminated. Generous severance packages can help soften this blow. For those who remain, special performance bonuses for help during the transition period can provide morale-boosting incentives.

The strategic plan of the acquiring firm will reduce uncertainty by providing a philosophical road map to the direction of the enterprise. Major changes undertaken by management will appear less capricious, easing the transition. Also, if employees understand the direction of the company, they can contribute more to implementation. For example, if staff employees understand the overall objectives and are asked to give specific suggestions about improving workflow or procedures, their reactions will be more responsive and their productivity is likely to increase.

The necessary job reductions should be approached with as much compassion as possible. One way of doing this is to make office services available to displaced workers. An outplacement officer can also be appointed to assist in the preparation of resumes, mailings, contacts with other companies, and other helpful services. Sometimes the use of early retirement offers can reduce the need for across-the-board job cuts. The most successful early retirement programs offer smaller actuarial reductions in retirement benefits, additional age or service credits, and other non-pension benefits such as one-time payments or post-retirement health care benefits. If the acquired firm has a stock option plan and the value of the stock of the acquired company increased as a result of the takeover, some of the key executives may be in a favorable position for early retirement. From the perspective of the acquiring firm, the expense of inducements in the early retirement offer is lowered by these stock market dynamics. It is sound business practice to treat displaced executives fairly. If they are angry about the treatment that they received, they may cause problems during the transition, either while operating from their homes or after they have relocated in a competing company.

Investing in the development and retraining of employees is especially critical in management ranks. This is true despite an organizational focus on downsizing. The need is clearly driven by changing corporate strategies, culture clashes, and organizational uncertainties. One way to approach this is to help managers move out of their "functional" mindsets and into a more organizational perspective. For example, managers from all functional areas can meet with the president of the company one day per week, with questions that have arisen during the week through interaction with their staff. These questions should range from the procedural to the philosophical. If the sessions are structured in such a way that the president responds to varied questions from the managers and discussion among the managers is encouraged, the managers will learn more about the entire organization and the mindset of senior management. Uncertainties will be resolved and managers can perform more effectively as a team.

Taking these extra steps when a company is acquired by another institution will help smooth the transition. They will help ensure that a single, integrated and focused culture can emerge and that trust and loyalty are preserved.

THE ART OF THE DEAL

The art of the acquisition deal is for the acquiring company to formulate its strategic plan. Then the firm must use its imagination and resourcefulness to identify the right target to accomplish specific aspects of that plan.

Selected References

Bird, A. and Israel, R. (1994) "Managing the Acquisition Process," *Strategic Planning*, May/June, 4–9.

Ernst & Young (1994) *Mergers & Acquisitions*. 2nd edn. New York: John Wiley & Sons.

Gutknecht, J. E. (1993) "Mergers, Acquisitions, and Takeovers: Maintaining Morale of Survivors and Protecting Employee," *Academy of Management Executive*, 7(3), 26–36.

Rock, M. L., Rock, R. H., and Sikora, M. (1994). *The Mergers and Acquisitions Handbook*, 2nd edn. New York: McGraw-Hill.

Smith, C. and Walter, I. (1997) *Global Banking*. New York: Oxford University Press.

3

ADDENDUM 3.1
HOSTILE TAKEOVERS IN EUROPE

In continental Europe, hostile offers were virtually unheard of before the 1980s. In this region, takeovers were not dominated by institutions and insiders often held concentrated holdings. This began to change during the 1980s as institutional holdings increased, markets improved and trading volume increased, and financial professionals from the USA became interested in European markets. By the end of 1995, many highly visible hostile takeover attempts had been launched in France, Italy, Sweden, Germany, Denmark, Spain, Ireland, Portugal, and Switzerland. After a number of hostile transactions, attitudes began to change. Attention was paid to the actual performance of target companies and the management teams that led them, to the position of minority shareholders in change-of-control situations, to the rules affecting disclosure of share accumulations, and to restrictions on voting shares acquired by unwelcome holders.

In 1991 the Amsterdam Stock Exchange limited the number of barriers to hostile takeovers that Dutch companies had relied on for years, and in 1992 it issued a warning to 20 listed companies that had not complied. Later in 1992, the chief of Germany's leading fund management company, a subsidiary of Deutsche Bank, called for a code of practice to permit and regulate contested takeovers in Germany. Similar actions have occurred in other parts of Europe.

Two Models

Since the Single Market Act and the various efforts at financial market reforms that have occurred in most of the principal European countries, attempts have been made by the European Union and member countries to devise a common set of takeover rules and procedures. In general, there are two approaches.

- The British model involves a set of rules designed to protect minority shareholders from unfair transactions. This system depends on full disclosure and procedures that follow established rules.
- The German model, though many other countries follow similar practices, protects the rights of major shareholders, such as banks and insurance companies. This system encourages firms to behave in a somewhat paternalistic manner to protect the interest of all shareholders.

Market and legal forces are eroding the viability of the German model, and Germans are still working toward a compromise between the two systems.

Regulatory Developments

Regulations that affect takeovers are numerous. These include antitrust regulations and securities laws or regulations relating to fraudulent practice – for example, required disclosures, trading restrictions (such as insider trading rules), and prohibitions against making false markets. There are also rules, codes, and established procedures prescribed by stock exchanges or by self-regulatory bodies that may or may not be supported by enforcement powers. These various tiers of regulation can be imposed at national as well as at the EU level. Until a few years ago they were vastly different from one another, creating a confusing and often uneven playing field for participants. Efforts have been made to harmonize regulations.

The European Union
Regulation at the EU level has so far been confined to the antitrust sector. There are two governing principles in effect.

- "Subsidiarity" (a concept of EU governance that extends into all aspects of the common market), which provides that the EU will make no decision on issues that can be decided equally well at the national level.
- "Compatibility with the common market," which restricts EU actions to matters affecting the whole of the EU.

The EU regulations that were passed in 1990 provide the following:

- Only deals involving combined worldwide sales of ECU 5 billion, or two or more companies with EU sales of euro 250 million, will be reviewed by the EU's "merger task force."
- The merger task force must report within one month after announcement whether it believes the deal is compatible with the common market.
- If the merger task force reports any doubts about the transaction, it has four months to resolve them and either approve the deal, block it, or insist on modifications.

At the national level, regulatory bodies such as Britain's Monopolies and Mergers Commission and Germany's Cartel Office rule on deals below euro 5 billion in size, and are required by national regulations to consider mainly national competitive effects. These bodies usually decide within a few weeks of an announced transaction whether they see a competition problem. If so, a more extensive review, for up to six months, is undertaken before the deal can be completed. During this period the bid is usually withdrawn, to be reinstated after the review if the buyer decides to do so.

The British Model

In terms of securities laws, there are also considerable differences. Under the British system, all share accumulations above a threshold of 3 percent of outstanding shares must be announced to the market. When a bidder accumulates 30 percent of the stock of the target, the bidder is obligated to make an offer to all other shareholders at the same price. Once a bid is announced, certain time schedules must be adhered to. The intent is to create a "level playing field" on which neither bidder nor defender would have any advantage over the other and on which the market could decide the outcome on a fair and unimpeded basis.

To ensure equity in the market transactions, the British system relies on the Takeover Panel, a non-government body staffed by professionals with a small permanent staff. The Panel has issued rules (the Takeover Code) that must be observed, previously only at penalty of sanction but now it is legally enforceable by the government. The Panel has the power to rule on disputes as they occur, and its decision is binding.

Lawsuits are only rarely involved. The process is generally regarded as flexible, timely, fair, and efficient. Though different in many details from takeover procedures in the USA, which rely mainly on court actions in the state of incorporation of the defending company, the basic principles and objectives are very similar. Moves to accommodate the Anglo-Saxon model have been made in France and a few other countries, and are the basis of the draft European Takeover Directive, which requires a statutory body to regulate mergers.

The German Model

A different system of corporate governance exists in Germany (and several other European countries) which tends to minimize the frequency of takeovers. In these countries, a two-tiered board system is used to govern corporate affairs. Companies are required to maintain a Supervisory Board, with no representation by management, but with representatives of labor unions, banks, local municipalities, and other interested parties. Often the chairman of the Supervisory Board is a senior official of the company's main bank (*Hausbank*). The main bank may own shares in the company itself, usually will have extended loans to the company, and also will have been given voting proxies by bank customers who own shares in the company. The bank will also maintain close contact with other financial shareholders and often act on their behalf. Accordingly, the Hausbank will have considerable power to wield over the conduct of the company's affairs.

The main duty of the Supervisory Board is to appoint members of the Management Board, all of whom are employees of the company. The Supervisory Board may also unilaterally decide to restrict the voting rights of certain shareholders, subject only to challenge by 50 percent of all shareholders. If management should misbehave or the company run into difficulty or be in need of restructuring, the Supervisory Board, led by its chairman, is expected to step in and put things right. As the principal shareholders are mainly financial institutions or other corporations, the assumption is that if the Supervisory Board acts in accordance with the interests of this inside group of investors, then the interests of lesser shareholders will be taken care of (such investors being seen sometimes only as free riders).

Thus, specific laws to protect minority shareholders are not needed and do not exist. Shareholdings need only be disclosed when they reach 25 percent of outstanding shares.

CHAPTER 4

IS A MERGER OR ACQUISITION THE RIGHT DECISION?

INTRODUCTION

The decision to participate in a merger or acquisition should be reached only after careful consideration of the alternatives and taking steps to minimize unpleasant surprises associated with the business combination. The basic question is whether the firm could more efficiently "build" the capacity rather than "buy" it through merger or acquisition. If the answer to this question is "No," due diligence can help determine the likelihood of future problems associated with financial, legal, or operational aspects of the merger candidate.

In other cases, beneficial aspects of working with another company can be realized without an actual merger. Other alternatives are:

- joint ventures
- strategic alliances
- minority investments
- venture capital programs, and
- licensing agreements

THE CASE FOR INTERNAL DEVELOPMENT

When expansion or diversification is considered, the first decision often is whether to "buy" or "build." The choice between internal development and acquisition is determined largely by the costs and benefits, including important opportunity cost factors that are often overlooked. These factors relate to the degree of "disturbance," or internal motivational dysfunction that might occur as a result of an acquisition.

An acquisition can be compelling because it is a short-cut to what is needed, but it is not the right decision for every company; nor is it appropriate for every project or program launched by a business. In fact, many highly successful firms avoid acquisitions entirely or rarely pursue them. Examples include:

- Minnesota Mining & Manufacturing (consumer and industrial products)
- Merck & Co. (in pharmaceuticals)
- Texas Instruments (semiconductors)
- Johnson & Johnson (health care products).

These companies have relied primarily on internal development to sustain strong track records.

Acquisition itself means that resources will have to be diverted from ongoing business activities to pay for the transaction. Since these resources could have been used for internal development, the existing organization might resist the use of resources for outside purchases, and management of existing businesses could lose motivation. Another potential threat to motivation is the disturbance that an acquisition necessarily creates in the ongoing business activities of a firm. New people must be integrated into the organization, new managerial assignments made, and new working relationships developed. These integration activities take time, create human tension, and expend organizational energy.

Just the fact that a firm is willing to pursue its strategies through acquisitions may have a negative impact on internal operations. The commitment to pursue new business through internal means sends a strong message to the organization that top management has confidence in the current personnel. Conversely, a strong negative message may be sent – with attendant negative motivational impact – when the firm oscillates between internal development and acquisitions. This pattern can amount to mixed signals to the operating personnel. In such an environment, a strong commitment to internal excellence must be fostered.

Nevertheless, even internally oriented firms do not exclude the possibility of mergers and acquisitions in their deliberations. Acquisitions can add new products and technologies, widen customer bases, bring in critical skills, help the company expand its geographic markets, and boost production capacity with almost lightning speed. Absorption of an entire organization can give the acquirer an instant advantage over competitors and generate immediate financial or technical contributions to the combined company. While purchases may involve large up-front expenditures, acquisitions can be more cost-effective than the *de novo* route. Paybacks are faster and the learning curve for start-ups can be eliminated.

However, these advantages disappear for many companies, especially large, well established firms that are geared to heavy investment in R&D, new product development, and capital spending to enhance productivity. These firms are typically on the cutting edge of technology. The advantages often also disappear for companies that already have large market shares. For these firms, acquisition would be an overkill and may elicit concerns about anti-trust (constraint of trade) issues. External opportunities will not materialize if there are seldom any businesses, people, plants, or processes outside the firm that are worth acquiring. In such cases, a firm is better served by developing technologies, launching new products, or moving into new geographic territories on its own initiative.

Even when the internal choice is not so apparent, many companies prefer internal development. For some, this approach is so embedded in their strategic plans that they have learned to live with and manage delayed paybacks and slower learning curves while producing respectable rates of return. Typically, these companies have developed unique skills in building new plants, developing new products, entering new territories, and recruiting critical personnel. These abilities cushion them from the most severe problems inherent in start-up projects. In a *de novo*-based strategy, an acquisition may be interpreted as overextending the investment capital pool.

Other reasons for opting for internal development include the following.

- Some companies dislike making large lump-sum payments and prefer staggering cash outlays in smaller increments over the term of a start-up.
- Competing with other firms in the M&A market for target companies repels many managements.

- Being forced to negotiate with managers in the target firm has no appeal for some firms.
- Some companies lack the skill or the inclination to integrate another business and its personnel into their organizations.

Timing can also play an important role in the decision to adopt the internal development approach. When the M&A market is highly competitive, many companies – including active acquirers – reject the high prices for potential acquisition targets as uneconomical investments.

DUE DILIGENCE

Once the decision has been made to merge with or to acquire a firm, a due diligence examination must be conducted. This involves examining every aspect of the proposed transaction to ensure that all relevant and material information is available to the parties.

Legal Foundation for Due Diligence in the USA

In the USA, the concept of due diligence has been codified by the Securities Act of 1933 – considered enlightened legislation because it sought to regulate by information. That is, rather than promulgate absurd rules that would dictate which firms could offer their securities to the public and which could not, the US Congress chose to leave that decision to the public investor. However, so that the investor can make an informed decision, the Act requires that a firm offering its securities to the public make a reasonable effort to disclose to potential investors all material information or be held liable for its absence. The responsibility for the due diligence investigation, together with financial liability, also extends to securities underwriters (investment bankers).

In the context of issuing securities, primary responsibility for the due diligence investigation generally falls on the investment bank that will subsequently manage the underwriting syndicate – called the lead underwriter, the lead manager, or the bookrunning manager. The potential liability associated with the due diligence investigation provides a powerful motivation for investment bankers to investigate fully and disclose all material information. Accountants and lawyers review in minute detail the financial statements and practices of the firm going back at least five years. The audited statements, together with the accountants' opinion letters, constitute an integral part of the process. If appropriate or warranted, the investment bank also does a thorough background check on all members of senior management. There may be one or more lengthy management interviews by the underwriter's counsel and anything suspect is researched and verified.

4

The disclosure of information required in the issuing of securities often results in a conflict between the investment bankers and the issuer's management, who are often the original owners – particularly in the case of an initial public offering (IPO). The managers, who built the business and never before had to account to anyone but themselves (except perhaps the tax authorities), suddenly find that they are required to disclose a great deal of information – information that they consider confidential and competitively sensitive.

Thus, while the investment banker is in the position of promoting a new securities issue, the banker always must be conscious of its responsibilities to present all material information in a fashion that is never misleading.

Due Diligence in a Merger or Acquisition

In a similar way, a firm that is acquiring another is obviously of the opinion that the firm has strong strategic advantages. At the same time, the acquirer must take appropriate steps to establish that there is no material omission of facts that might change the expectations of the business combination. The process of ensuring that an individual or entity is an appropriate and suitable partner for any business transaction is also referred to as due diligence.

The objective of the due diligence process is to obtain information about the target firm, thus enabling the acquirer to reach an educated conclusion. The results of due diligence efforts help the decision maker(s) better assess the business risks of the transaction and negotiate the transaction.

Figure 4.1 provides a sample checklist of information to obtain and issues to address during the due diligence examination. The satisfactory completion of the examination will provide added assurance that the merger or acquisition or acquisition proposal is sound.

FIGURE 4.1

Due Diligence Checklist

I. **Financial information**
   A. Annual and quarterly financial information for the past three years:
      - income statements, balance sheets, and cash flows, including footnotes;
      - planned versus actual results;
      - management financial report;
      - breakdown of sales and gross profit by:
         - product type
         - distribution channel
         - geography;
      - current backlog by customers;
      - accounts receivable aging schedule.
   B. Financial projections:
      - quarterly financial projections for the last two fiscal years and the latest quarter; revenue by product type, customers and channel (full income statements, balance sheets, cash flow statements);
      - major growth drivers and prospects;
      - predictability of business;
      - risks attendant to foreign operations (e.g. exchange rate fluctuation, government instability);
      - industry and company pricing policies;

FIGURE 4.1 Continued

- economic assumptions underlying projections (different scenarios based on price and market fluctuations);
- explanation of projected capital expenditures, depreciation, and working capital requirements;
- external financing arrangement assumptions.

C. Capital structure:
- current shares outstanding;
- schedule of all options, warrants, rights, and any other potentially dilutive securities with exercise prices and vesting provisions;
- summary of all debt instruments/bank lines with key terms and conditions;
- off balance sheet liabilities;
- capital losses.

D. Other financial information:
- summary of current federal, state, and foreign tax positions, including net operating loss carryforwards;
- general accounting policies (revenue recognition, etc.);
- schedule of financing history for equity, warrants, and debt (dates, investors, dollars investment, percentage ownership, implied valuation, and current basis for each).

II. **Products**
A. Descriptions of each product within each market segment (including product literature).
B. Major customers and applications.
C. Historical and projected growth rates.
D. Market share.
E. Speed and nature of technological change.
F. Timing of new products and product enhancements.
G. Cost structure and profitability.

III. **Customer information**
A. Representative list of 20 customers – names, addresses, phone numbers, products owned, and timing of purchasers.

4

FIGURE 4.1 Continued

B. List of strategic relationships (contact names, phone numbers, revenue contributions, marketing agreements).

C. Revenue by customer (names, contacts, and phone numbers of any customers accounting for 5% or more of revenue).

D. Brief description of any significant relationship severed within the last two years.

IV. Competition

Description of the competitive landscape within each market segment including the following:

A. Market position and related strengths and weaknesses as perceived in the marketplace.

B. Basis of competition (e.g. price, service, technology, distribution).

V. Marketing, sales, and distribution

A. Strategy and implementation:
- discussion of domestic and international distribution channels;
- positioning of the company and its products;
- marketing opportunities/marketing risk;
- description of marketing programs and examples of recent marketing/product/public relations/media information on the company.

B. Major customers:
- status and trends of relationships;
- prospects for future growth and development.

C. Principal avenue for generating new business.

D. Sales force productivity model:
- compensation
- average sales quota
- sales cycle
- plan for new hires.

E. Ability to implement marketing plan within current and projected budget.

VI. Research and development

A. Description of R&D organization:
- strategy

FIGURE 4.1 Continued

- key personnel
- major activities.

B. New product pipeline:
   - status and timing
   - cost of development
   - critical technology necessary for implementation
   - risks.

C. Patents:
   - dependence on outside licensing and patents;
   - patents currently held by the company.

D. Relationships with third parties:
   - joint R&D efforts
   - participation in industry associations.

E. Ability to implement marketing plan within current and projected budgets.

VII. Management and personnel

A. Organization chart.

B. Historical and projected headcount by function and location.

C. Summary biographies of senior management, including employment history, age, service with the company, years in current position.

D. Compensation arrangements:
   - copies (or summaries) of key employment agreements;
   - benefit plans.

E. Discussion of incentive stock plans.

F. Significant employee relations problems, past or present.

G. Personnel turnover:
   - data for last two years;
   - key unfilled vacancies.

VIII. Legal and other matters

A. Pending lawsuits against the company – details concerning claimant, claimed damages, brief history, status, anticipated outcome, and name of the company's counsel.

B. Pending lawsuits initiated by the company – details concerning defendant, claimed damage, brief history, status, anticipated

---

FIGURE 4.1 Continued

outcome, and name of the company's counsel.

C. Description of environmental and employee safety issues and liabilities:
- safety precautions
- new regulations and their consequences.

D. List of material patents, copyrights, licenses and trademarks – issued and pending.

E. Summary of insurance coverage/any material exposures.

F. Summary of material contracts.

G. History of regulatory agency problems, if any.

IX. **Other company information**

A. Business plan, if available.

B. List of board members.

C. List of all stock holders with shareholding, options, warrants, or notes.

OTHER ALTERNATIVES TO MERGERS AND ACQUISITIONS

For a variety of reasons, a merger or acquisition may not be the best way to accomplish linkage with another company. Other alternatives include:

- joint ventures
- strategic alliances
- minority investments
- venture capital programs
- licensing agreements.

Joint Ventures

Corporate partnering has become increasingly popular. The most common form is the joint venture in which two or more firms join forces to create a new jointly owned business entity for a specific purpose. These joint ventures have been driven by financial, industry-specific, techno-logical, and geographic forces. However, despite potentially great eco-nomic advantages, these combinations often are fraught with problems that invariably are tied to corporate cultural differences. Unfortunately, many ventures actually fail to accomplish their intended goal because of governance conflicts or culture clashes.

Essentially, a joint venture allows businesses to pool various types of resources for common gain. A major drawback from the onset is that nei-ther firm receives 100 percent interest in the joint venture or 100 percent of the profits from the joint venture. This issue must be addressed at the time the joint venture agreement is reached to avoid subsequent prob-lems associated with partnership stakes.

Variations of the joint venture include:

- start-up business
- near merger
- cross-border joint venture
- sale of a peripheral division, and
- financing joint venture.

Start-up Business

A common type of joint venture is, in essence, a start-up business devised to develop a new technology, to commercialize products from newly developed technologies, or to enter new markets. Each partner brings skills, knowledge, and resources to the venture that it would have needed to acquire if the venture had not been formed. In addition, a joint project may be advisable to spread the high costs of technological advancement or to acquire complementary resources. IBM, Texas Instruments, Apple Computer, Du Pont Co., and Corning, Inc. are among the technology-centered companies that have formed joint ventures with both technology and non-technology firms to accomplish strategic devel-opment. For example, Corning, derives about half of its sales and earn-ings from technology-type joint ventures that leverage Corning's skills in the glass and ceramic fields.

Near Merger

A second type of joint venture, sometimes referred to as a near merger, combines existing subsidiary businesses of two or more companies. The objective is to enhance market presence. Such partnerships frequently are forged in mature industries in which the partners have relatively small market shares but want to become part owners of a larger enterprise. B. E. Goodrich and Uniroyal combined their tire businesses in efforts to create a stronger competitor to industry leader Goodyear Tire & Rubber.

The near merger approach also has been used in growth markets.

- General Mills and Nestle joined forces to effect worldwide expansion of their cereals businesses.
- General Mills also entered a joint venture with the Frito-Lay division of PepsiCo, Inc. to create a strong presence in the European snack food market.
- Eastman Kodak contributed its Sterling Drug subsidiary to a joint venture with Sanofi of France to create the research and marketing "critical mass" needed to compete in the global and increasingly high-cost pharmaceutical business.
- Merck & Co. and Johnson & Johnson formed a joint venture in over-the-counter pharmaceuticals, linking Merck's research prowess with Johnson & Johnson's marketing skills.

Cross-border Joint Venture

Numerous tie-ups involve cross-border joint ventures, that is, ventures between companies situated in different countries. On entering a new country, a foreign firm frequently will take on a local partner that knows the territory and is willing to contribute financially. The Toys 'R' Us chain in Japan is a joint venture between Toys 'R' Us of the USA – supplying the retailing concepts and skills – and McDonald's Japan – with its expertise in acquiring store sites in Japan where land is scarce.

There are numerous variations on the cross-border joint-venture theme. Joint ventures may be substitutes for acquisitions. When Philips of the Netherlands wanted to move its test and measurement instruments operation into the USA, it set up a reciprocal distribution venture with John Fluke Manufacturing, an American firm that makes similar products. Markets have widened for both firms as Fluke distributes the Philips lines through its established distribution system in the USA while Philips distributes Fluke products in Europe.

Sale of a Peripheral Division

4

In a variation that combines elements of acquisitions and venturing, a joint venture can be created when a company sells part interest in a subsidiary to another business. Philips sold the Whirlpool Corp. of the USA a major stake in its home appliance business, which provided the American firm with entry into overseas markets. In some cases these deals may be the first step to complete acquisition by the "investor." This was the case with Whirlpool – it eventually bought out Philips' remaining interest in the appliance business.

Financing Joint Venture

A financing joint venture is one in which two or more companies team up to buy an operating business. The objective is either to spread the cost or to dissolve the jointly owned businesses at some future time and distribute specific assets to the partners that want them most. For example, when Loral Corp., the defense supplier, bought the Ford Aerospace unit of Ford Motor Company, Loral took Lehman Brothers as a partner to help defray the purchase price of more than $1 billion.

Joint Venture Governance

In all forms of joint venture, structure and governance systems are important. Ideally, the venture should be set up as an independent company, especially if there is 50/50 ownership. Autonomy makes it possible for the company to be flexible enough to make decisions concerning its planning and operations without having these decisions cleared through one of the parent companies. Any personnel from the parent companies should sever ties with the parent and work under separate work contracts and benefit plans. Everything possible should be done to ensure a new corporate culture in the joint venture firm.

Winding Up a Joint Venture

Many managers view joint ventures as marriages. The metaphor is an attractive one and in many ways appropriate. As with a marriage, the success of a joint venture depends on committed partners who communicate honestly and openly.

However, the analogy is also dangerous. It has led many managers to fall prey to a fallacy that the termination of a joint venture, like the termination of a marriage, is a sign of failure. On the contrary, termination is a natural outcome for most joint ventures. The end of a joint venture is not necessarily a sign that it has failed, even if its life span has been short. It may mean simply that the business logic for the venture no longer applies.

In many ventures, for example, a foreign partner provides a particular product or skill in return for the local partner's expertise and access to markets. Such partnerships typically end once the entrant has developed its own understanding of the market or the market has opened up to direct foreign competition.

In other cases, companies enter into ventures as a way to evaluate a particular market or technology. In the biotechnology industry, for example, large pharmaceutical companies often invest in ventures with smaller companies that possess promising new technologies. If the technologies materialize, the larger partner may acquire the venture, providing a healthy cash infusion to the smaller partner, but, at the same time, terminating the original joint venture.

Yet even though termination is a natural event in the joint venture life cycle, parent companies often fail to plan for it when they are setting up their ventures. Frequently, managers spend a considerable amount of time on the formative decisions, such as selecting partners and allocating operating responsibilities. They often overlook the termination considerations and, when the venture must be wound up, there may be no mechanism in place to guide the process.

To avoid this situation, explicit pricing provisions may be built into joint venture agreements. One of the partners may, for instance, negotiate an option to either purchase or sell the venture at a mutually agreed price. The option can be exercisable on a specific date or triggered by an event, such as the passage of foreign-investment legislation.

Another approach is to write in a "shotgun" clause. This type of clause permits one partner to stipulate a price at which the other partner must either sell or acquire the venture.

Apart from pricing mechanisms, there are other ways that parent companies can smooth the eventual termination of a joint venture. They can write into the venture agreement procedures for reviewing performance, arbitrating disputes, and allocating resources and property rights. Parent companies should also consider the impact of a terminated venture on their businesses. An acquiring parent will want to ensure that the venture can be absorbed into its existing organization, and a divesting parent will want to minimize any disruptions from the loss of the venture.

Joint ventures are often transitory structures. One of the best ways to ensure a venture's success is to reach clear agreement at the outset on the venture's graceful cessation.

STRATEGIC ALLIANCES

Strategic alliances are difficult to define because they take so many different forms. However, it is generally agreed that a strategic alliance between two companies creates a framework for a long-standing business relationship. Such alliances may lead subsequently to joint ventures on specific projects, technology sharing, marketing agreements, and other developmental approaches. Despite the variety of strategic alliances, the joint venture principles of establishing common goals and values and avoiding culture clashes – especially critical in cross-border settings – are important in forming successful alliances.

Supplier Alliances

For many companies, alliances with suppliers provide a unique opportunity to enhance overall company performance without a formal stakeholding. Companies that take the time to cultivate better supplier relationships can negotiate better prices and delivery times. In this way, opportunities are created for both sides to innovate, leading to improved performance.

When building strong supplier relationships, the most important factor is to include key strategic suppliers early on – developing joint objectives to meet business goals. This requires partnering on a wide range of initiatives including the knowledge and use of alternative technologies, supply chain integration, prototype and design support, creative thinking, international ventures, and process improvement.

Canadian grocery giant National Grocers and multinational retailer WalMart are good examples. These firms have been successful in building strong supplier relationships by working closely on inventory management and replenishment.

Supplier relationships create competitive advantage most readily when the CEO makes the relationship a priority. To be successful, companies need to develop partnership programs that directly support their overall business goals such as shareholder value creation and revenue growth.

Industry leaders can develop tailored supply strategies that are directly linked to their corporate strategies. These companies are able to use their supplier relationships as a true source of competitive advantage across their business. They use suppliers to maximize their own products' competitiveness, going beyond the narrow focus of cost reduction.

Unfortunately, few companies achieve a level of trust with their suppliers necessary to partner on key process management. Firms are reluctant to share sensitive information with their suppliers. Other barriers include comfortable relationships with existing suppliers, providing little incentive to investigate cost savings or innovative opportunities outside of current practices and relationships. Also, companies may have inadequate data to analyze, monitor, and control systems; and many firms lack experience managing major improvement programs.

Nevertheless, strategic alliances with suppliers can result in almost immediate benefits. There is an established business relationship and a built-in incentive for both parties to succeed.

Technology and Marketing Alliances

4

Contractual alliances are less formal and involve less commitment because the partners do not form a new corporate entity separate from the parent organizations, as they do in a joint venture. Two of the most popular types of functional alliances are technological and marketing alliances.

■ Technological alliances involve cooperation in upstream value chain activities such as research and development, engineering, and manufacturing.

■ Marketing alliances involve cooperation in downstream value chain activities such as sales, distribution, and customer service.

Technological alliances often involve the production and sharing of knowledge. As a commodity, knowledge entails two major problems, externality and property rights, which lead to high transaction costs in a market-based, fee-for-service transaction. Strategic alliances help reduce these costs.

Marketing alliances are typically formed when products enter the mature or declining phase of their life cycles. Thus, marketing alliances appear to have a shorter horizon of benefits than technological alliances which are concentrated in the early stages of the product life cycle.

Firms entering strategic alliances may also experience asymmetric resource dependence. Small start-up firms are often sought out as alliance partners because of their access to technological expertise and research abilities. Accordingly, large firms often are more dependent on small firms for technological expertise than vice versa.

Firms enter different types of strategic alliances with varying motives.

Technological alliances become necessary in high-technology industries where the rapid pace of frontier technology development, product complexity, and the high cost of product development make cooperation beneficial to even the most sophisticated company. Apart from providing incentives for investing in R&D without duplication, technological alliances, compared to mergers and acquisitions, help firms reduce transaction costs, protect knowledge from expropriation, and ease the transfer of tacit (often unspoken) knowledge.

Another benefit of technological alliances is that of cost advantages. Fixed costs in a cooperative project may be lower than in an individual effort because of (1) economies of scale and scope, and (2) sharing of overhead expense.

Marketing alliances are different from technological alliances in scope and benefits. In marketing alliances, the major source of benefit is stimulation of demand. Possible forms of cooperation in such alliances are cross-selling products, sharing brand names, advertising, or promotion; distribution channels, sales forces, or sales offices; and marketing and service networks. Such alliances, particularly ones with a distributor or a complementary product manufacturer, can give manufacturers entry into new geographical markets or customer segments, thereby increasing product demand. As in joint ventures, alliance partners' market development activities may encourage new infrastructure development for manufacturing and distribution in entirely new industries, resulting in demand growth.

MINORITY INVESTMENTS

Several large companies, especially in technology- or research-intensive fields, maintain active programs for taking minority positions in smaller businesses. Typically, the investee company is a small firm, public or private, that is working on a leading edge technology or product but needs a cash infusion to move forward. The larger company provides the funds in return for positions on the board and other rewards.

The Basic Concept

The intent of the investment seldom is to acquire the investee. Rather, many minority investments take on features of strategic alliances in which the investor company is interested primarily in manufacturing or marketing rights to the products or processes being developed.

In such a case, a minority investment may be preferable to an acquisition. The price of the minority investment usually is much cheaper, which mitigates risk, and if the investee is in a developmental stage, it is probably difficult to value. Perhaps most importantly, companies with active minority investment programs appear to have a vested interest in encouraging investee companies to maintain an entrepreneurial spirit – a spirit that could be stifled if the small firm were incorporated into a corporate bureaucracy. (As with all other corporate development initiatives, minority investments require considerable study before commitments are made.) Many investees remain stand-alone companies, and some have gone public with large returns for the investors. Among the companies with wide-ranging minority investment activities are Eastman Kodak; IBM; Pfizer, Inc.; AT&T; and SmithKline Beecham.

The presence of a minority investor has other benefits. The minority investor also can be an intervening force that insulates the investee company from being taken over unwillingly.

Minority Investment by Japanese Firms in the USA

Partial ownership can take the form of a foreign investing firm's sharing equity in a new company with individual investors who are usually officers in the new company, rather than sharing equity with existing manufacturing corporations. Typically, the partially owned firm makes a product that was designed or partially manufactured by the foreign investor.

Japanese ownership of manufacturing facilities in the USA is a sensitive political issue. The decline of such basic industries as steel, machine tools, consumer electronics, and automobiles has been tied to an increase in sales of facilities to Japanese companies. Consequently, many Japanese companies favor investment alternatives other than total ownership in highly visible industries such as steel and automobile production.

Two factors may contribute to the visibility of a company in the target industry.

- Its industry may be politically sensitive, a condition often accompanied by the presence of import protection, as is the case in the auto and steel industries.
- The reputation of a parent company or companies may increase an entity's visibility.

The visibility of firms also increases with their size. For large ventures, equity positions by Japanese firms may be more desirable than total ownership, as the partial stakes imply that Japanese parents are investors rather than owners.

Joint ventures represent some loss of control for Japanese parents. A partial equity position also represents a loss of control in firms in which Japanese parents

- have patents;
- have a proprietary technology for the product produced or the process used; or
- provide major components.

In such instances, a joint venture is a compromise between control and political sensitivity and between total ownership and partial equity. Thus, the Japanese partial investments in the USA, which are usually in high-tech industries, are not true joint ventures because individual investors hold substantial blocks of the stock.

The use of this equity structure and the growth in total ownership by Japanese firms suggest a learning effect not previously analyzed. There was usually a relationship before a firm was formed. In many cases, a US investee previously imported products from the Japanese parents. Such firms may have been started to add value to imported products or to position assembly or fabrication closer to the point of demand. The benefit of eventual technology transfer might actually outweigh the reduction in manufacturing and transportation costs.

Joint ventures are preferred and more prevalent when the Japanese parents make similar products in Japan. The data supports the proposition that joint ventures are favored in industries threatened with trade restrictions and in which a seasoned (by a competitive home market) Japanese investor enters. Joint ventures are preferred when a new entity is created.

Thus, minority investments can have political advantages that are not shared with acquisitions. If an industry is politically sensitive, a minority investment can reduce the opposition to foreign investments. Also, minority investments can be used to improve cross-border business relationships to enhance product quality or customer service.

VENTURE CAPITAL

Venture capital investing by large companies is related to minority investments. The major difference is that investees are more like prototypical venture capital-backed start-ups that have high promise but no track records. Venture-capital investments ease risk through relatively small commitments and let investees operate as entrepreneurial businesses.

The company with a venture capital program, typically sets it up as a separate unit, staffed by experienced venture capitalists familiar with the risks and rewards. The staff have the analytical skills required to reach a decision about a potential investee.

Many of the most successful high-tech companies are applying management models used by venture capitalists to find and fund good ideas quickly. Corporate management at many high-performing electronics companies manage their business units much as venture capitalists manage their portfolios. The key elements of the corporate venture capital model include the following.

- *Setting a company-wide vision, but ensuring the autonomy of business units.* This is comparable to the portfolio philosophy in corporate acquisitions (see Chapter 1). Senior corporate management sets the company-wide vision, ensuring that each business unit's goals are consistent with the firm's corporate strategy. Corporate management also looks at investment opportunities across the company and determines which business unit initiatives represent the best use of corporate assets. Business unit plans are often evaluated in terms of profit potential, strategic benefits, cross-unit leverage, potential cannibalization, and other considerations.

- *Hiring the best business unit management and motivating them with performance-based compensation.* While corporate management sets the vision, business units are charged with finding the best way to implement that vision. The process works most effectively when management sets clear and consistent goals and employs performance-based compensation practices like stock options to reward business unit performance.

- *Providing for a dynamic re-allocation of company resources when opportunity knocks.* By staffing the business units with top management talent, corporate management demonstrates its commitment and strives to foster an entrepreneurial environment in the business units. Corporate management also employs more flexible capital allocation methods to help fund good projects as they arise, without waiting for annual budget cycles. By shifting funds from profitable, established business units to promising new opportunities in the same or other business units, corporate management is better able to optimize the performance of the entire firm.

The new venture capital model is relevant for high-technology companies because it shifts responsibility for finding and developing new business opportunities to the business units that are closest to the market. This model allows companies to respond at market speed, exploiting new opportunities as they arise.

Companies can achieve the benefits of business acquisitions, that is, receive infusions of expertise and technology without engaging in full integration of two firms. Venture capital programs can capitalize on the developments of small, entrepreneurial firms. Alternatively, a company can use the venture capital model and encourage development of similar competitive advantages internally.

4

LICENSING AGREEMENTS

Licensing is a versatile corporate development device for adding value to an asset or increasing cash flow streams. Licensing techniques are prominent in technology industries such as electronics, computers and computer peripherals, and pharmaceuticals. A company may license another business to use a patent or a proprietary product or process and receive royalties from the licensee. The technique can speed the payback from an expensive development and widen distribution in far-off markets with little or no investment. Of course, the *quid pro quo* is that the licensing firm must surrender a part of the returns.

Licensing also allows the developing firm to establish an especially strong process or technology breakthrough as the standard for its industry. This permits the firm to enhance its position in its primary markets.

Licensing also can be used for names and trademarks. Rights to names can be licensed to firms in foreign countries; or they can be granted to firms outside the licensing firm's core business. Apparel manufacturers, for example, frequently license their brand names for clothing items they do not produce.

THE RIGHT DECISION

The right decision to expand business opportunities may not be a merger or acquisition. It may be internal development. Or it may be one of several other alternatives: a joint venture, a strategic alliance, minority investments, a venture capital program, or a licensing agreement. In any event, the firm must conduct a comprehensive due diligence examination.

Selected References

Aulakh, P. S., Cavusgil, S. T., and Sarkar, M. B. (1998). "Compensation in International Licensing Agreements," *Journal of International Business Studies*, Second Quarter, 409–419.

Berlin, M. (1998) "That Thing Venture Capitalists Do," *Business Review: Federal Reserve Bank of Philadelphia*, January/February, 15–26.

Champion, D. (1998) "Joint Ventures: Planning for the End Game," *Harvard Business Review*, July/August, 21.

Das, S., Sen, P. K., and Sengupta, S. (1998) "Impact of Strategic Alliances on Firm Valuation," *Academy of Management Journal*, February, 27–41.

Frerichs, R. N. (1998) "Learning from Venture Capitalists," *Electronic Business*, February, 11.

Harbert, T. (1998) "Venture Capital Firms Place Their Bets on High Tech," *Electronic Business*, May, 5.

Lach, J. S. (1998) "What's the Outlook for Venture Capital Fund Performance?" *Trusts & Estates*, March , 67–70.

Lapidus, K. S. (1998) "Venture Capital and Rule 144: The Chilling Effect of Securities Regulation on Venture Capital Investing," *Securities Regulation Law Journal*, Spring, 75–116.

Llaneza, V. A. and Garcia-Canal, E. (1998) "Distinctive Features of Domestic and International Joint Ventures," *Management International Review*, First Quarter, 49–66.

Marshall, J. F. and Ellis, M. E. (1994) *Investment Banking & Brokerage: The New Rules of the Game*. Chicago: Probus Publishing Company.

Selz, M. (1998) "Here's the Problem – A Software Company Faces Dwindling Resources, Growing Competition, and Internal Turmoil; What Should It Do?" *Wall Street Journal*, March 30.

Swan, P. F. and Ettlie, J. E. (1997) "US–Japanese Manufacturing Equity Relationships," *Academy of Management Journal*, April, 462–479.

Tait, D. (1998) "Make Strong Relationships a Priority," *The Canadian Manager*, Spring, 21 and 28.

ADDENDUM 4.1
INTERNATIONAL JOINT VENTURES

The nationality of partners is not the only difference between domestic and international joint ventures. The decision to choose a domestic or international partner is influenced by the goals sought with the alliance. There are significant differences between the two types of joint ventures. The recognition of the distinctive features of domestic and international joint ventures allows the identification of the managerial problems affecting these companies.

The basic reasons for setting up joint ventures are as follows.

■ *Improvement of efficiency.* The creation of a joint venture permits greater efficiency in the performance of certain tasks. This efficiency may derive from economies of scale and scope which are difficult to accomplish by a single firm, from the spreading of risks among partners, as well as from synergies which stem from complementary resources provided by the partners.

■ *Learning or access to knowledge.* In joint ventures every partner has access to the knowledge and skills of the others. For example, when entering foreign markets, a local partner provides the joint venture, among other things, good knowledge of the special needs of customers, available channels of distribution or the political situation.

■ *Political factors.* Political factors which require or make it advisable to cooperate with local firms are frequently the reason for international joint ventures. Such is the case when a foreign firm wants to enter countries with hostile governments and/or restrictive legislation.

Generally, international joint ventures have been associated with the ability to enter new countries. Joint ventures were originally recognized as an alternative to wholly owned subsidiaries in the expansion of multinational firms. A joint venture in the international arena reduced the amount of transactions costs vis-à-vis wholly owned subsidiaries.

A firm faces two needs: it must be able to obtain resources from other partners (which leads to cooperation) and it must be able to protect the assets associated with their distinctive competencies (which leads to expansion through wholly owned subsidiaries). Thus, joint ventures are often considered the second best option in internationalization of the company.

The reasons for joint ventures are generic motives of cooperation, because the goals sought through the formation of joint ventures can be achieved through other contractual arrangements. There is no need for several firms that are willing to cooperate to set up a new entity, owned by them, to coordinate the activities for which the cooperation has been started. They can sign a contractual agreement which includes the rights and obligations of the parties and regulates the relations among them, without creating a new firm. That is why the features which characterize both domestic and international joint ventures are also determined by the propensity to create joint ventures over contractual agreements.

It has been suggested that joint ventures are chosen as contractual forms to organize cooperative activities of some complexity. This proposition is based on the fact that, in the case of simple alliances, the parties can govern the relationship by means of contracts without incurring the additional costs which derive from joint ventures – the set up and running costs of a new entity, legally independent from the partners. Two types of complexity have an influence on the propensity to form joint ventures, although to different degrees depending on the nationality of the partners.

- In international agreements, the most influential factor in the formation of joint ventures over contractual agreements has been *strategic complexity*: the need to learn about the characteristics of the local market of at least one of the partners. Thus the performance of the joint activities overlaps with the transfer of knowledge.
- In domestic agreements, the most influential complexity has been *organizational* – the number of partners and the scope of the activities,

aspects which make difficult the global tasks of coordination and control.

There are important differences among international joint ventures, differences that are a normal consequence of their uniqueness. They are created mainly to help a company penetrate new markets. In fact, while in domestic joint ventures the partners may want to seek collusive practices, access the technological know how of the others, or penetrate new sectors, international joint ventures are usually motivated by the desire of, at least one of the partners, to use the agreement as a means for international expansion. It is this circumstance that gives international joint ventures their particular characteristics.

4

- International joint ventures are characterized by a small number of partners (with an average number close to two). In general, a high number of partners increases the complexity of the agreement because it is more difficult to reach a consensus among them. Thus, the agreement will not have more than two partners unless some advantage is obtained from the addition of new partners. In this sense, the small number of partners in international agreements is attributable to the fact that a sole partner is usually enough to expand internationally: the right partner will provide all necessary information about the political, economic, social and cultural conditions of the country, and provide access to the local channels of distribution.
- The existence of policies restricting foreign investment can oblige the joint venture to have only one local partner. On the contrary, when objectives such as collusion, R&D activities, or economies of scale more suitable for domestic agreements are targeted, the participation of more than two partners makes it possible to reach more ambitious goals. But a higher number of partners also increases the complexity of the alliance, and, for this reason, the adoption of the joint venture as a contractual form can be more appropriate.
- Domestically, a low number of partners is more likely to result in a strategic alliance. The greater number of partners in domestic joint

ventures could also be explained by the fact that two-party domestic strategic alliances have a lower level of complexity, and thus there is a lower propensity to form two-partner joint ventures.

■ There is a less balanced distribution of equity in international joint ventures, particularly in those created in less developed countries. The distribution of equity in a joint venture is usually the result of the distribution of the negotiating power. In this sense, in domestic joint ventures the negotiating power is usually more balanced. Domestic joint ventures often are created with partners of a similar size. On the contrary, international joint ventures are usually formed by firms considerably different in size, in particular when the partner belongs to a less developed country – a traditional example is a multinational firm with a local partner. There is also another factor contributing to the unequal equity: several host governments – particularly in less developed countries – impose restrictions on the percentage of equity that multinational firms can own. This circumstance explains the predominance of unequal equity ventures in less developed countries.

■ Because they have a higher number of partners, domestic joint ventures will find it more difficult to establish their goals and strategy, as a greater number of interests must be harmonized. A consensus among partners about the strategy of the venture is necessary but the existence of a dominant partner does not make it easy. The problems that arise in international joint ventures are directly related to the additional complexity introduced by different nationalities of the partners. On the one hand, different nationalities can cause problems if the different cultures of the partners prove incompatible. On the other hand, a joint venture implies the intervention to a greater or lesser degree of the local government, restricting the activities of the foreign partner. It is also important, in international joint ventures, for partners to reach a consensus about objectives and strategy. When there are difficulties in achieving consensus, conflicts can arise. One factor that can create conflicts of interest in international joint ventures is the desire of multinationals to control. Nevertheless, the greater negotiating power of multinational firms, linked to their technical superiority and greater size, greatly mitigates these conflicts.

In summary, there is a different profile for domestic and international joint ventures, which is a consequence of the different motivation behind each type of joint venture.

4

THE SCIENCE AND ART OF VALUATION

INTRODUCTION

Once a merger or acquisition candidate has been identified, the business combination will be judged a success or a failure based on two criteria.

- Were the companies able to integrate their operations to achieve the synergies anticipated?
- Was the deal appropriately priced or did the acquirer pay too much?

The first question is addressed in Chapter 2 and Chapter 3. This chapter addresses the second question.

5

Valuing a firm is both science and art. Once projected cash flows have been estimated, the value of these future cash flows can be handled scientifically with techniques such as discounted cash flows, internal rate of return, and net present value. Net present value also can be adjusted to value the firm from the sole perspective of the equity holders (stock holders).

However, before projected cash flows can be estimated, many factors must be considered. Consideration of these factors constitutes the art of valuation.

THE ACQUIRING FIRM AND VALUATION

Merger and acquisition activity is driven by four types of buyers:

- domestic strategic buyers
- foreign strategic buyers
- financial buyers
- distressed property buyers.

Each type of buyer has its own perspectives on pricing. When an acquisition is priced, especially in competitive situations, it is critical to understand the types of competing buyers and how these competitors might make their pricing decisions.

Domestic Strategic Buyers

A typical domestic strategic buyer is interested in acquisitions that improve financial returns by strengthening its competitive position, while expanding its operations. Acquisitions often can provide a means for growth and expansion, and most importantly, increased market share. For example, these goals can be achieved by:

- acquiring a distribution channel, customer base, or new technology;
- capitalizing on the goodwill associated with an acquired trade name; or
- defensively, preventing a competitor from acquiring the same target and gaining its advantages.

Some strategic acquisitions are undertaken to meet corporate portfolio diversification objectives. A company whose profitability depends on a single business segment or product line often seeks to reduce its risk of exposure by entering other markets. It was this diversification mentality that, through mergers and acquisitions, led to the formation of numerous multi-industry conglomerates in the 1960s and 1970s. Far-reaching diversification strategies have not been as popular in the 1990s because many of the previously formed conglomerates were not successful.

A key factor in many strategic acquisitions is an acquirer's synergy expectations. Synergies come in the form of:

- cost reductions
- strategic position improvements, and
- financial benefits.

Cost reductions can be realized from staff rationalizations, removing redundant non-personnel overheads, and utilizing excess capacity. Strategic improvements can include realizing economies of scale, achieving critical mass in a particular market, or improving leverage with customers and suppliers. Financial synergies include tax benefits such as utilization of net operating losses (to reduce taxable income of the combined firm) and possible enhancements that reduce the cost of borrowing (lowering the cost of capital for the combined firm).

Strategic buyers usually have long-term investment return criteria and may be willing to wait as long as ten years to realize the benefits from an acquisition. However, if the strategic buyers have public stock holders, long-term objectives may be less important than short-term earnings dilution. Thus, amortization of goodwill would be unattractive. Moreover, strategic buyers want to protect credit ratings, are wary of capital expenditure, and resist other cash flow effects that could reduce a company's stock price. Valuation of the acquired firm will be reduced to the extent that credit ratings are an issue, large capital expenditures are necessary, or any other negative cash flow dynamic is present.

5

Strategic buyers also face concerns regarding the meshing of the corporate cultures of existing and acquired businesses. Extremely different corporate cultures can seriously damage or delay the realization of synergies and reduce the price paid for the acquired firm.

Foreign Strategic Buyers

Foreign strategic buyers (that is, overseas-based operating companies) have objectives similar to those of domestic strategic buyers, including expansion or enhancement of existing operations. Similarly, if they already have businesses within the host country, foreign companies can look to potential synergies. Most often, the overseas-based strategic buyer has a long-term focus as it grows businesses outside its home market. Some seek a strategic foothold to achieve global expansion plans and consider acquisitions to be quicker and more economical than developing operations from scratch in the host country.

Foreign buyers with public stock holders have shareholder and stock price concerns similar to their host-country counterparts, but they may have less concern over short-term earnings dilution. A foreign buyer also may benefit from different financing considerations, such as government support, that can enable it to pay more for an acquisition than a domestic competitor. Capital market influences in the country of the foreign company – such as the cost or availability of debt or equity financing –

can significantly change the attractiveness of an acquisition to a foreign entity. If favorable capital market conditions exist in the foreign country, the acquirer can afford to pay more for the targeted firm.

At the same time, foreign buyers face complicating foreign exchange and tax issues, including the optimal timing of a purchase and the repatriation of earnings. Finally, a prospect of regulatory interference or negative publicity sometimes can cause foreign buyers to abandon aggressive acquisitions programs, especially in sectors that might be politically sensitive.

Financial Buyers

The typical financial buyer consists of a group of individuals organized to invest a pool of institutional funds in the purchase of businesses, while financing these transactions on a leveraged basis through borrowing. The buyers repay debt from the operating cash flows of the acquired businesses. Once debt has been substantially reduced, financial buyers sell the business either privately or to the public through an initial public offering (IPO). Financial buyers do not face the same shareholder concerns that typically confront strategic buyers such as earnings dilution, but they are responsible to their investors who expect high returns.

Since financial buyers are principally in the business of buying and selling companies to generate investment returns, their investment objectives and expectations differ from those of strategic buyers. Financial buyers typically have expectations of annual returns of 30 to 40 percent, exiting the investment in three to seven years. Rate of return and exit objectives are constrained by terms that must be negotiated with lenders. Lenders impose constraints that affect the price paid, including required debt-to-cash-flow coverage ratios and specified periods over which debt must be paid before dividends can be declared.

Financial buyers are more likely to invest in mature businesses because such companies generate the steady cash flow necessary to ensure debt repayment and have minimal capital expenditure and working capital requirements. Financial buyers also look for companies in which there is a potential for cost reductions to improve cash flow. These opportunities could include reductions in overhead or divestiture of non-core assets.

Distressed-property Buyers

Distressed-property buyers comprise a small group of acquirers who share traits of both strategic and financial buyers. The distinguishing feature of these buyers is that the businesses they seek are typically in trouble, ideally allowing an acquirer to pay a bargain price and gain value by effecting a turnaround. They are willing to confront the complexities of financial workouts and the issues connected with bankruptcy proceedings – such as varied interests of trade creditors, secured and unsecured lenders, and the complex set of tax rules that apply.

It should be noted that distressed-property buyers can include strategic acquirers seeking inexpensive properties, although most are financial buyers who need very little equity capital. The proliferation of distressed-property buyers reflects a dramatic increase in companies facing bankruptcy, beginning in the late 1980s and early 1990s.

Thus, the prospective buyer and its objectives will play a role in determining the price of an acquisition. These differences translate into adjustments that should be made to projected cash flows. The challenge is to capture the relevant aspects of the deal and to subject them to the science of valuation.

VALUATION PRINCIPLES

The science of valuation is based on discounted cash flow techniques. Among these techniques are:

- payback period
- internal rate of return

- net present value, and
- profitability index.

Payback Period

The payback period is the oldest method of evaluating investments and the easiest to apply. Payback period is the expected length of time for positive cash flows to equal the price of the acquisition, or the time it is expected to take to recover the price. The payback period is an intuitively appealing approach in that it is easy to understand. It also has the advantage of giving some insight to the estimated time during which the investment will be "at risk."

Internal Rate of Return

The internal rate of return (IRR) is the rate that causes the price of the acquisition to exactly equal the present value of the projected future cash flows. Unlike payback period, the IRR is a function of both the amount of the cash flows and their timing. In applying the IRR technique, the objective is to find the rate that will satisfy the condition of equality between the present value of projected cash flows and the price of the acquisition.

$$\text{Price of Acquisition} = \sum_{t=1}^{n} \frac{(CF_t)}{(1 + IRR)^t}$$

Net Present Value

Net present value is the difference between the present value of the future cash flows (using the appropriate discount rate) and the price of the acquisition.

$$NPV = \left(\sum_{t=1}^{n} \frac{(CF_t)}{(1 + k)^t} \right) - \text{Price of Acquisition}$$

Central to the determination of net present value is the appropriate discount rate, k. This rate should reflect investors' rate of return on the next best investment alternative. As such, k is a minimum required rate of return for the acquisition. Conceptually, the bracketed term in the NPV equation represents the value of acquisition to the acquiring firm. The price of the acquisition is the required cash outlay to obtain the target firm. If the value of the acquisition exceeds the required cash outlay, value is added to the acquiring firm.

Since maximization of shareholder wealth is the objective of financial management, the measurement of change in shareholder wealth that is directly attributable to specific acquisitions makes net present value a decidedly useful technique. When the value of the acquisition is more than the price of the acquisition, an increase in shareholder wealth of the acquiring firm can be realized. When the reverse is true – that is, the value of the acquisition is less than the price of the acquisition – the purchase of the company will lead to a decrease in shareholder wealth for the acquiring firm.

Profitability Index

Profitability index (PI) is the ratio of the present value of the projected future cash flows (using the appropriate discount rate) and the price of the acquisition. The profitability index is related to NPV. NPV is the difference between acquisition value and cost. Profitability index is the ratio of acquisition project value to cost.

$$PI = \frac{\sum_{t=1}^{n}\left(\frac{(CF_t)}{(1+k)^t}\right)}{\text{Price of Acquisition}}$$

Since PI measures value of the project per dollar of initial investment:

■ PI will be greater than 1 whenever the value of the acquisition exceeds its price;

- if price and value are equal, PI will equal 1;
- PI will be less than 1 if the value of the acquisition is less than its price.

THE SCIENCE OF VALUATION: DISCOUNTED CASH FLOW (DCF)

Value as an Ongoing Concern

Discounted cash flow (DCF) valuation of a firm involves determining the value of a stream of cash flows that do not end. This is the value of the firm as an ongoing concern, that is, the acquirer purchases a time series (into infinity) of free cash flows that are generated by the assets purchased.

DCF valuation uses a discount rate that reflects the firm's weighted-average cost of capital or the price it must pay to suppliers of both debt and equity capital. Accordingly, the cash flows are developed independent of financing costs.

Likewise, any required increases in working capital or anticipated capital expenditures must be deducted. If cash flow must be retained in the business, it should not be included in the valuation. Such cash flows create no incremental value for the acquiring firm.

Thus, in valuing a going concern with existing liabilities, the after-tax cost of interest is added back to accounting income to create an unlevered (without debt) cash flow. Also, required increases in working capital and capital assets are deducted. It is this series of cash flows that, when discounted to the present, represents the economic value of the firm on a stand-alone basis. Cash flow in any given year is defined as follows:

Free cash flow = Net income + noncash expenses
+ interest expense (net of tax)
– capital expenditures
– net increases in working capital

Finding a Terminal Value

As noted above, DCF valuation methodology attempts to value the company as a going concern into infinity. However, in practice, projections for firm valuation typically are not carried out to 20 years and certainly not to infinity. Accordingly, DCF valuation is separated into two components:

- a forecast of free cash flows for a number of years;
- a terminal value that approximates the present value of the free cash flows that occur in the years after the end of the forecast period.

Typically, pro forma financial statements are prepared for five to ten years and then a terminal value.

Terminal value at the end of the period of cash flow forecasts may be arrived at in different ways. Three of the methods are:

- estimating book value at the terminal date;
- applying a price/earnings multiple to forecasted earnings – either net income or earnings before interest and taxes (EBIT);
- equating the terminal value to the present value of a perpetual stream of cash flows that begin the year after the terminal date – assuming a constant rate of growth.

Terminal book value is estimated by projecting the balance sheet forward to the last year of the forecast horizon and arriving at the book value of the common equity account at that time. It is assumed, under this scenario, that the interim free cash flow has been paid out.

A terminal price/earnings or EBIT multiple essentially values the firm at the end of the horizon in the same way that the stock market would value it – by capitalizing the then-current earnings. The choice of the proper multiple will, obviously, have a large effect on the terminal value, and care should be taken to choose a multiple consistent with the characteristics of both the industry and the company at that time. It would be inappropriate, for example, to use a high P/E at the end of the horizon for

115

a company that was forecasted to have stable margins and relatively low growth rates.

The third way of estimating a terminal value, equating terminal value to the present value of a growing stream of cash flows, is slightly more complicated but conceptually more consistent with the premises of DCF valuation. In essence, this technique multiplies the free cash flow in the last forecasted year (or a "normalized" free cash flow if there is something unusual about that year's cash flow) by a multiplier that estimates the value of the cash flows in perpetuity. The terminal value is:

$$\text{Terminal Value} = FCF_t \left[\frac{(1 + g)}{(k - g)} \right]$$

where g = assumed rate of growth of cash flow stream into the future

k = weighted average cost of capital

FCF_t = free cash flow in year t, the last forecasted year

This formula capitalizes a stream that is growing at g percent into the future and the stream is discounted at k percent.[1] Because of the assumptions underlying the model, the value of this stream is as of the end of the projected period – that is, as of period t.

In practice, one analyzing the value of a firm may use all three of these terminal value estimation techniques in an attempt to cross-check each method. Doing so permits greater confidence in the terminal value estimate.

---

[1] This calculation is based on the Gordon constant growth model. The numerator is the free cash flow estimated for the first year after the forecasted period. Note that it has grown at the rate of g, as will all other cash flows in the projected stream. The cash flow is then divided by the difference between the discount rate and the constant rate of growth. The result is the value of all cash flows from the first year after the forecasted period through infinity.

Combining Forecasted Period and Terminal Value

Once the series of free cash flows (up through the end of the forecasted period) and terminal value are estimated, the present value of these two components is calculated. An acquirer is paying today for access to the cash flows generated by the assets in the future. Thus, these flows must be discounted to the present.

5

Cost of Capital

The appropriate discount rate is the marginal weighted average cost of capital (WACC):

$$WACC = w_D k_D (1 - t) + w_P k_P + w_E k_E$$

where WACC = weighted average cost of capital
k_D = marginal cost of debt
k_P = marginal cost of new preferred stock
k_E = marginal cost of common equity
w_i = weight of capital component i
= percentage of total capital represented by capital component i
t = corporate income tax rate

Practically speaking, the weighted average cost of capital is never used as a point estimate of the "right" discount rate. Instead, the calculation defines the center of a range of discount rates (usually one to two percentage points on either side of the estimate) that will be used to discount the cash flows.

It should be noted that the appropriate WACC is that of the acquiree, not that of the acquirer. Why not use the buyer's weighted-average cost of capital? Essentially, the acquiree's cost of capital captures the inherent risk associated with its assets and, thus, the uncertainty regarding the timing and the magnitude of the cash flows generated by those assets. Another way to think of this is that the cost of capital of the acquired firm is the price it must pay to the suppliers of capital to motivate them to invest in that company. Thus, the acquirer's cost of capital focuses on the wrong combination of risks in constructing a discount rate.

Sensitivity Analysis

Those who analyze a prospective merger devote a large portion of their time to performing sensitivity analyses on a DCF valuation. The DCF is only as accurate as the assumptions underlying it, and the most direct way to delineate the margin of error is by varying the assumptions. This involves designing different operating or financial scenarios for the company and noting the results. Sensitivity analysis always focuses on the key line items that most affect the valuation.

Throughout the sensitivity analyses, the range of discount rates is held constant. The discount rate reflects the risk associated with the assets. That is, the range of WACC accounts for the variability in the timing and magnitude of the cash flows. The result of the sensitivity analysis is a range of values for the company or assets in question.

THE ART OF VALUATION: QUALITATIVE ISSUES

Valuing mergers and acquisitions goes beyond DCF valuation. Qualitative issues are used in connection with DCF valuation to make the valuation as comprehensive as possible. In some instances, acquisition values will be quite similar to DCF values. In other instances, they may be quite different. Acquisition value requires the incorporation of knowledge and assessment of:

- comparable precedent transactions
- corporate strategies
- business economics and special circumstances
- points of view of actual and potential participants.

Two concepts are important in incorporating the qualitative aspects of a business combination:

- market for corporate control
- market premiums.

Market for Corporate Control

Business valuation attempts to estimate how a company will "trade" in the market for corporate control. The obvious starting point is current stock market trading levels for a publicly held firm. For a privately held company, the analyst attempts to estimate at what price the company would trade if it were publicly traded. The valuation of privately held companies can be estimated – within reasonably tight parameters – through comparison with similar public companies and by analyzing the financial and business characteristics of the firm in question. The value of a company in the market for corporate control usually is higher (and often much higher) than its value in the secondary trading market.

The reason for this is linked to the word "control." Essentially, control of assets and the ability to direct all of the free cash flow generated by assets are worth more to a business manager, than participation in a small percentage of a business – without control – is worth to the individual stock holder.

Market Premiums

Market premium is a concept that commands much attention. The amount above the market trading level of the target company's stock is a derived figure rather than an analytical tool or concept. The DCF analysis, as well as other considerations, can justify acquisition values over current secondary trading levels.

The decision to pay a premium must rest on the conclusion of the analysis and should not itself be a valuation exercise. DCF values and comparable transaction multiples, adjusted for specific factors, offer a much more consistent explanation of values paid in control transactions than a history of premiums paid over stock-price levels.

Nevertheless, market premium is a useful concept in assessing how a potential acquiree or its shareholders may react to a specific proposal. In fact, if no premium is offered, many transactions have little likelihood of success, regardless of the validity of the valuation analysis supporting the buyer's proposition. A major exception to this general rule is in the merger of equals share-exchange deal, which involves little or no premium to either side.

FIGURE 5.1

Cost of Capital

$$\text{WACC} = w_D k_D (1 - t) + w_E k_E$$

$$0.15 = (0.40)(0.1136)(1 - 0.34) + (0.60)(0.2000)$$

where WACC = weighted average cost of capital
w_D = % of total capital composed of debt
w_E = % of total capital composed of equity
k_D = before-tax cost of debt
t = tax rate

EQUITY RESIDUAL METHOD

All of the calculations of merger or acquisition value have used the weighted average cost of capital (WACC) as the minimum required rate of return. This rate satisfies all suppliers of capital. The WACC is a product of the capital structure of the firm (the composition of the right-hand side of the balance sheet) and the cost of the components of capital, as illustrated in Figure 5.1. The following assumptions are used:

- 40 percent of capital of the firm is contributed by debt holders;
- 60 percent of capital is contributed by common equity holders;
- on a pre-tax basis, the cost of debt is 11.36 percent;
- the tax rate is 34 percent;
- on an after-tax basis, the cost of debt is 7.5 percent [0.1136(1 – 0.34)];

- the cost of equity (always higher than the cost of debt because of the lower priority of equity claims) is 20 percent;

Under these assumptions, the weighted average cost of capital is 15 percent.

Whenever net present value has been computed using this WACC, the implication is that debt holders are exactly satisfied in terms of their minimum required rate of return. Likewise, common shareholders have also been satisfied. When net present value is exactly zero, both contributing entities earn exactly their minimum required rates of return. To the extent that net present value is positive, there is then an excess return that accrues only to shareholders.

An alternative way to compute net present value is the equity residual method in which cash flows that will accrue to debt holders are included in the cash flow stream. These cash flows are then discounted at the appropriate equity rate of return. The value of an acquisition using the equity residual method can be determined by assuming one of two types of debt service cash flow patterns:

- bond-type debt service
- installment debt service.

Bond-type Debt Service

The equity residual method can be applied by assuming that debt-holders receive cash flows that are equivalent to bond payments of interest and principal, that is, a bond-type debt service. Using a hypothetical acquisition target, we note that a $100 investment of debt and equity will return operating cash flows in the six-year life of the project of $35, $15, $42, $37, $22, and $60 (the terminal value), respectively, as shown in Figure 5.2.

Assuming that the debt is 40 percent of this investment, $40 will be contributed by debt holders in period zero. This implies a required investment by equity holders of $60. In each of the next six years, according to this method, interest on the debt must be paid at an 11.36 percent pre-tax rate

---

FIGURE 5.2

Alternative Net Present Value, Equity Residual Method, Bond-type Debt Service

Project A:

Year	0	1	2	3	4	5	6
Operating CF$_s$	(100)	35	15	42	37	22	60
Debt service[1]	40	(3)	(3)	(3)	(3)	(3)	(43)
Equity residual	(60)	32	12	39	34	19	17

[1] The financing for the acquisition was 40% debt and 60% equity. The before-tax cost of debt is 11.36%; the after-tax cost is 7.5%. Each year, interest on $40 is paid ($40 × 0.075 = $3) as well as the principal repayment in year 6.

---

with a 34 percent tax rate, that results in an after-tax cost of debt of 7.5 percent. Since 7.5 percent of $40 is $3, this interest payment reduces the operating cash flows in each of the six years. The principal of $40 is repaid in year 6, bringing total debt service in that year to $43. Thus, from the

---

FIGURE 5.3

Alternative Net Present Value, Equity Residual Method, Bond-type Debt Service

Conventional NPV

$$
\begin{aligned}
NPV &= 35/(1.15) + 15/(1.15)^2 + 42/(1.15)^3 + \\
&\quad\ 37/(1.15)^4 + 22/(1.15)^5 + 60/(1.15)^6 - 100 \\
&= 30.4348 + 11.3422 + 27.6157 + \\
&\quad\ 21.1549 + 10.9379 + 25.9397 - 100 \\
&= \underline{\underline{27.43*}}
\end{aligned}
$$

Equity Residual Method

$$
\begin{aligned}
NPV &= 32/(1.20) + 12/(1.20)^2 + 39/(1.20)^3 + \\
&\quad\ 34/(1.20)^4 + 19/(1.20)^5 + 17/(1.20)^6 - 60 \\
&= 26.6667 + 8.3333 + 22.5694 + \\
&\quad\ 16.3966 + 7.6357 + 5.6933 - 60 \\
&= \underline{\underline{27.30}}
\end{aligned}
$$

perspective of equity holders, the price of the acquisition of $60 will generate cash flows in the six-year period of the project of $32, $12, $39, $34, $19, and $17, respectively.

Figure 5.3 shows the computation of net present value (NVP) using the conventional approach and the equity residual method. The conventional calculation of NPV (using WACC) results in $27.43.

On the other hand, NPV using the equity residual method incorporates only the net cash flows that accrue to equity holders. These cash flows are discounted at 20 percent, the equity rate of return. The resulting net present value is $27.30. In this case, the result is quite similar to the NPV using the conventional approach.

5

FIGURE 5.4

Alternative Net Present Value, Equity Residual Method, Installment Debt Service Cash Flows

Project A:

Year	0	1	2	3	4	5	6
Operating CFs	(100)	35	15	42	37	22	60
Debt service[1]	40	(8.52)	(8.52)	(8.52)	(8.52)	(8.52)	(8.52)
Equity residual	(60)	26.48	6.48	33.48	28.48	13.48	51.48

$$
\begin{aligned}
\text{NPV} \ = \ & 26.48/(1.20) + 6.48/(1.20)^2 + 33.48/(1.20)^3 + \\
& 28.48/(1.20)^4 + 13.48/(1.20)^5 + 51.48/(1.20)^6 - 60 \\
= \ & 22.0667 + 4.5000 + 19.3750 \\
& + 13.7346 + 5.4173 + 17.2405 - 60 \\
= \ & \$22.33
\end{aligned}
$$

[1] The financing for the acquisition was 40% debt and 60% equity. The before-tax cost of debt is 11.36%; the after-tax cost is 7.5%. If annual installment payments are made, these payments are subtracted to arrive at the equity residual.

Installment Debt Service

The result in Figure 5.3 under the equity residual method is related to cash flows that are attributable to debt service. Should those cash flows be significantly different, the net cash flows to equity holders will also be different. Figure 5.4 presents an alternative situation. The operational cash flows of the acquisition target are the same. However, in this case, debt service is assumed to be in the form of an amortizing annuity, that is, installment debt service. Each payment includes interest on the outstanding debt and principal repayment. While each payment is equal, the composition of interest and principal reduction changes over time.

In period zero, the net cost of the project for equity holders is the same $60, as in Figures 5.2 and 5.3. The difference is that all the debt-service cash flows in years 1–6 equal $8.52.[2] This provides a different stream of future cash flows to the equity holders. When these cash flows are discounted at the 20 percent rate that is applicable for equity providers, the net present value is $22.33.

The equity residual method, whether bond-type or installment, can be used whenever the emphasis is on the actual return to equity holders. If debt service requirements are known with certainty or if debt service is considered a part of doing business, as in the case of a bank or other financial institution, the equity residual method may be preferable. Essentially, the focus shifts from satisfying all suppliers of capital to focusing on the return to the supplier of equity funds.

---

[2] At the after-tax interest rate of 7.5 percent, six payments of $8.52 each will exactly repay the $40 borrowing.

THE ART AND THE SCIENCE

Valuation of mergers and acquisitions is based on accepted principles of finance – especially DCF methods. This is the science of valuation. However, the projection of free cash flows, decisions concerning cost of capital, conducting sensitivity analyses, estimating the appropriate premium (if any), and other aspects of valuation call for considerable artistry on the part of the firms involved.

5

MULTINATIONAL ACQUISITIONS

INTRODUCTION

There are a number of reasons for a company to consider an overseas operation. The firm may wish to take advantage of sales potential in that region. Alternatively, a manufacturer may enter an overseas market to obtain raw materials that are not available in the domestic market. In some cases, there may be production efficiencies that can be realized in other countries but not in the domestic market. For example, low-cost labor can attract manufacturing operations to overseas locations. In other cases, overseas technology may be superior in a particular industry. Any one or a combination of these reasons can motivate expansion into a foreign market. Whatever the motivating reason, acquisitions in foreign countries must be analyzed from the same perspective as domestic projects, that is, whether they are financially feasible.

FIGURE 6.1

Multinational Diversification – Critical Issues

- Foreign currency exposure
- Political risk
- Parent versus affiliate cash flows

CRITICAL ISSUES FOR INTERNATIONAL ACQUISITIONS

International acquisitions are characterized by important distinguishing features and the following issues must be considered:

- foreign currency exposure
- political risk
- parent versus affiliate cash flows.

Foreign Currency Exposure

The most basic element of risk that is introduced in the context of multi-national operations is the exposure of domestic operations to changes in foreign currency exchange rates. Assume that the parent company is domiciled in the USA. When assets of the parent are denominated in a foreign currency, the primary risk for the domestic firm is a decline in the dollar value of foreign currency. Conversely, when liabilities are denominated in a foreign currency, the primary risk for the domestic firm is that the dollar value of foreign currency will increase.

FIGURE 6.2

Foreign Currency Rates – the Japanese Yen

Yen value of a dollar
¥106 = $1
[106 ¥/$]

Dollar value of the yen
¥106 = $1
¥1 = $1/106
¥1 = $.00943396
[0.00943396 $/¥]

With the exception of the British pound sterling, most exchange rates are stated in terms of the foreign currency value of one US dollar (US$1). As illustrated in Figure 6.2, this is also true for the Japanese yen. The yen value of $1 is stated as 106 which means that ¥106 = $1. For US investors and US multinational firms, the dollar value of the yen is more relevant than the yen value of a dollar because most financial results for these entities are reported in terms of US dollars. Since consolidated reports of assets, liabilities, and income are denominated in terms of US dollars, it is more intuitively appealing to think of foreign currency transactions in US dollar terms. In this way of thinking, foreign currency is just another commodity that has a specified dollar value. As also illustrated in Figure 6.2, the exchange rate of ¥106 = $1 means that each yen has a dollar value of $0.00943396.[1]

When Assets are Denominated in Foreign Currency

Assume for a moment that a firm has an asset, for example, accounts receivable, denominated in yen. Assume further that the amount of the receivable is ¥100 million and that it is due in 60 days. At the current exchange rate of ¥106 = $1, this receivable currently has a value of $943,396.

$$¥1 = \$0.00943396$$

$$¥100,000,000 = \$943,396$$

However, this receivable may or may not generate $943,396 when collected. If the exchange rate changes to ¥110 = $1, the company will receive substantially fewer dollars at the time that the receivable is collected.

$$¥110 = \$1$$

$$¥1 = \$0.00909091$$

$$¥100,000,000 = \$909,091$$

If the exchange rate changes in this way, the company will receive $909,091. This is $34,305 less than the original amount of the accounts receivable. Thus, when a US company has an asset denominated in a foreign currency, the element of risk is that the dollar value of the foreign currency will decline. Equivalently, the risk is that the foreign currency value of the dollar will increase.

---

[1] To convert an exchange rate from the foreign currency value of a dollar to the dollar value of foreign currency, divide both sides of the equation by the number of foreign currency units per dollar. In this case, both sides of the equation are divided by 106.

When Liabilities are Denominated in Foreign Currency

If the firm has a liability that is denominated in foreign currency, for example, accounts payable, the foreign exchange risk is exactly the opposite to the above. If we again assume that the US company's payable is in the amount of ¥100 million, the firm is obligated to pay $943,396 at the originally stated exchange rate of ¥106 = $1. However, if the exchange rate changes, the dollar equivalent of this yen liability will also change. For example, if the exchange rate goes to ¥100 = $1, the company will actually end up paying $1 million to satisfy this liability.

$$¥100 = \$1$$

$$¥1 = \$0.01$$

$$¥100,000,000 = \$1,000,000$$

In this case the difference is $56,604. When a liability is denominated in a foreign currency, the element of risk is that the dollar value of the foreign currency will increase. If the dollar value does increase, more dollars are required to satisfy the same liability. This is also equivalent to a decrease in the foreign currency value of a dollar.

Foreign currency exposure can be controlled, if not eliminated. Hedging mechanisms can be used to protect short-term exposure to foreign currency. Foreign currency hedging instruments include foreign currency futures contracts, currency options, and currency swaps.

Political Risk

Political Risk Defined

Political risk is not as easily quantified as foreign currency exposure, but it is just as real. The most extreme form of political risk is the risk of expropriation. Expropriation is the seizure of private property by the government. In some cases, expropriation will be compensated, but the amount of compensation may not be negotiated on completely arms-length terms. For example, the host government may insist on compensating the foreign company in something other than a hard currency.[2] In such a case, the foreign currency exposure is obvious. There may also be some question as to the true value of the investment. If the government uses book value, that is, depreciated book value, as a barometer of the value of an investment, this valuation may be substantially below the fair market value of the assets of the firm.

Expropriation is the most extreme form of political risk, but not the only form. It is also politically risky to operate in a country in which the government is not stable. Each sovereign government outlines the rules of operation of all commercial enterprises. If changes in government are not orderly, it is possible that the rules of business operation will change radically and unpredictably. In such a case, it is difficult to anticipate the correct long-term strategies. Examples of this kind of political risk are the collapse of the Soviet Union and the 1989 civil unrest in the People's Republic of China in Beijing's Tiananmen Square.

Protecting Against Political Risk

To guard against political risk, it is possible to purchase insurance through national-government and multilateral agencies. In the USA, the Overseas Private Investment Corporation (OPIC), is a government agency that provides insurance against various forms of political risk. These risks include expropriation, war, revolution, insurrection, civil strife, and loss of business income. In addition, OPIC provides protection for US investors in foreign countries for conversion of their dividends and other foreign currency cash flows into dollars.

The Multilateral Investment Guarantee Agency (MIGA) of the World Bank Group provides insurance for foreign investors and actively works to develop dialogue between the international business community and

---

[2] Hard currencies are those that are traded world wide and for which there are readily available contracts in the spot (immediate exchange) market and in currency derivative markets. Hard currencies are generally recognized to include the US dollar, British pound, German mark, Japanese yen, French franc, and Swiss franc.

host governments. Thus, there are mechanisms that can be used to control exposure to both foreign currency risk and political risk.

Parent versus Affiliate Cash Flows

The third critical issue in making international acquisitions is the form of financial analysis. There are two filters in deciding on a foreign acquisition. The first is finding the value of the subsidiary in the host country, net of the price paid for the acquisition. This is the net present value of the acquisition in the host country and is based on affiliate cash flows.

In the context of international acquisitions, evaluation of the net present value of the acquisition in the host country is still necessary, but not totally sufficient. An added element that is equally important is an analysis of cash flows to the parent company. This means that, in addition to the customary valuation, it is also necessary to evaluate cash flows that will actually flow to and from the parent company.

CASE STUDY: A PROPOSED INVESTMENT IN THE PEOPLE'S REPUBLIC OF CHINA

Consider a proposed acquisition by Allied Electronics, a hypothetical US firm.[3] Allied has an opportunity to invest in the People's Republic of China (PRC). The investment would involve setting up a subsidiary in Quangdong Province. The proposed acquisition will involve starting a new company – Hsu Electronics.

The proposed arrangement is for Allied Electronics to operate the Chinese electronics firm for five years. At the end of five years, the affiliate will be sold to private Chinese investors. The Chinese government has

---

[3] The structure of this example follows the outline provided in Eiteman, D. K., Moffet, M. H., and Stonehill, A. I. *Multinational Business Finance*, 8th edn. Addison Wesley; Chapter 18.

agreed to make special concessions for Allied because it is particularly interested in attracting high-technology foreign investment. The special provisions include relatively low income tax rates during the five years of operation and no capital gains tax when the venture is sold at the end of this five-year period. These concessionary provisions are consistent with the Chinese government's ambition to increase the level of technological competence within the Chinese economy. The Hsu Electronics venture is particularly appealing to the government. However, the sale of the project at the end of five years is not optional – the firm must be sold to Chinese investors.

Chinese Exchange Rates and Inflation Rates

Allied has already determined that the value of the Chinese currency, the Renminbi, will decline over time. This decline is anticipated because of the relatively high inflation rate in China as compared to the USA. As shown in Figure 6.3, the depreciation of the Renminbi will amount to a 7.5 percent decline in the dollar value of the foreign currency each year.

FIGURE 6.3		

Projected Exchange Rates – Chinese Renminbi

Because of differential inflation rates in the People's Republic of China and the USA, the Renminbi is expected to decline in value by 7.5% per year. The current and projected exchange rates are as follows.

Year		Rmb/$	$/Rmb
0	[5.772306]	5.772306	0.173241*
1	[5.772306(1.075)]	6.205229	0.161154
2	[6.205229(1.075)]	6.670621	0.149911
3	[6.670621(1.075)]	7.170918	0.139452
4	[7.170918(1.075)]	7.708737	0.129723
5	[7.708737(1.075)]	8.286892	0.120672

* Represents initial exchange rate.

FIGURE 6.4

Anticipated Price Level Changes

Price changes	% per annum
Hsu Electronics sales price	10.0
Chinese raw materials	4.0
Chinese labor wages	12.0
US general price level	2.5

Figure 6.4 contains information concerning anticipated price fluctuations in the People's Republic of China. The price of the products to be manufactured by Hsu Electronics will more than likely increase at the rate of 10 percent per year. The price of Chinese raw materials, on the other hand, will not increase as quickly. This rate of inflation for raw materials is expected to be on the order of 4 percent. However, in order for the standard of living of Chinese workers not to deteriorate in the face of high general price level increases, labor wages are projected to increase at the rate of 12 percent per year. All of the anticipated Chinese price level changes are substantially in excess of the average US inflation rate that is anticipated – 2.5 percent. These differential inflation rates will have significant impact on the estimation of cash flows attributed to the proposed Hsu Electronics facility.

FIGURE 6.5

Proposed Acquisition of Hsu Electronics by People's Republic of China

- **Sales**

  Sales in the first year of this five-year investment are projected at Rmb50 million. Sales in each subsequent year will increase by 6% in terms of volume. The price level will increase by 10% per year.

- **Working capital**

  Working capital (cash, accounts receivable, and inventory) must be maintained at the level of 25% of sales. All working capital needs must be financed by parent company Allied Electronics. The enterprise will require an initial working capital investment of Rmb10 million.

- **American components**

  Allied will export components to Hsu from the USA. The cost of these components to Hsu will increase by 6% in terms of volume, but only by 2.5% in terms of price level (US inflation rate). The cost of these components to Allied is 80% of the cost to Hsu.

- **Chinese raw materials**

  The cost of Chinese raw materials will increase by 6% in terms of volume and 4% in terms of price level.

- **Labor costs**

  While labor costs will also increase by 6% in terms of volume, increases in price level will be 12% per year.

- **Licensing fees**

  Allied will receive licensing fees of 1% of sales per year, tax-deductible in the People's Republic of China, but taxable income in the USA.

- **Taxes**

  The Chinese corporate income tax rate is 40% and the US rate 34%.

- **General and administrative expense**

  General and administrative expense will not fluctuate with sales, but will increase by 2% per year.

- **Depreciation**

  Plant and equipment will be depreciated over its ten-year life on a straight-line basis, with no anticipated salvage value.

6

FIGURE 6.5 Continued

- **Dividends**

  Dividends will be paid to Allied on the basis of net income. One-half of net income may be paid in this manner with the rest being devoted to working capital needs.

- **Project Cost**

  The company will require an initial capital investment of Rmb15 million.

- **Terminal Value**

  At end of five years, this electronics company will be sold to private Chinese investors for Rmb20 million, subject to neither Chinese nor US taxation.

An Overview of the Project

Figure 6.5 gives a summary of the important details of the Hsu Electronics proposed company.

Sales

The project itself should generate Rmb50 million in sales during the first year of operation. Because the Chinese economy is growing at a healthy pace, sales in terms of volume will increase at 6 percent per year. At the same time, the price level of these projects should increase at the rate of 10 percent per year.

Working Capital

To support this level of sales, working capital is required in the amount of 25 percent of sales. Working capital includes cash, accounts receivable, and inventory. These are normal ratios for Allied in their domestic operations and they are anticipated to be the same for the Chinese project. Because of the rather limited resource markets in China, it is anticipated that the working capital must be financed either through direct investment by Allied Electronics or through reinvestment of operational cash flows after project initiation. The start-up working capital that will be required, and must be financed by the parent company, is Rmb10 million.

Component Parts Bought from the Parent

A large number of the components for the products to be manufactured in China will originate from the Allied facilities in the USA. Because of the anticipated 6 percent increase in volume each year, the need for these components will also increase at the rate of 6 percent. However, because the components are manufactured in the USA where the inflation rate is lower, the price level increases are expected to be only 2.5 percent. Furthermore, 20 percent of the price of the components paid by Hsu Electronics represents gross profit for Allied.

Raw Materials

Raw materials will increase by the same 6 percent in volume as sales because raw materials usage is directly related to the level of production and sales. Price increases for raw materials are anticipated to be 4 percent per year.

Labor

The cost of labor will increase at the 6 percent rate because it, too, varies directly with the level of production or sales. The rate of inflation for labor costs will be a substantially higher 12 percent per period.

Licensing Fees Paid to Parent

Licensing fees are to be paid by Hsu Electronics. Such fees are to compensate for the transfer of technology from the US parent company to the Chinese affiliate. The licensing fees will amount to 1 percent of sales per year. Such licensing fees are tax deductible by Hsu in the PRC and represent taxable income for Allied in the USA. Increases in licensing fees will be proportional to increases in the level of sales.

Taxes

Taxes in the PRC are generally higher than those in the USA. The Chinese government has permitted a preferential tax rate of 40 percent of corporate income in the case of the Hsu Electronics project to encourage technology investments by foreign firms. The income tax rate in the USA is 34 percent for corporations.

General and Administrative Expenses

General and administrative expenses include salaries for managers, occupancy expense, office equipment expense, utilities to operate the office facilities, and insurance. Such expenses are expected to be relatively stable but will increase slightly by an anticipated 2 percent per year.

Depreciation

The Hsu Electronics plant and equipment will depreciate over a ten-year anticipated life on a straight-line basis, with no anticipated salvage value. As is true in the USA, depreciation expense is deductible for the purposes of Chinese income tax calculations.

Dividends to the Parent

Allied Electronics as the parent company and owner of 100 percent of the stock of Hsu Electronics will receive dividends from the Chinese subsidiary. These dividends will be in the amount of one-half of the net income of the operation. The remaining portion of income will be retained in the business to meet working capital and other needs.

Plant and Equipment

In order to establish the necessary plant and equipment, Allied Electronics must invest Rmb15 million. At the end of five years, the company will be sold to private Chinese investors.

Terminal Value

The terminal value or predetermined sale price will be Rmb20 million.

This Rmb20 million cash flow to the parent company will not be subject to Chinese or US taxation. In exchange for this predetermined compensation, Allied will relinquish all rights to working capital, plant, equipment, patents and copyrights developed during the five-year period within Hsu Electronics. However, this buy-out at the end of five years will not preclude Allied from participating in a subsequent joint venture with Hsu Electronics.

Rates of Growth in Cash Flow

Figure 6.6 contains the calculation for annual changes in the cash flows for various elements of the analysis. The calculation of the correct rate of increase is determined by reference to the Fisher Effect.

FIGURE 6.6

Hsu Electronics – Specific Rates of Change in Revenue and Expense

$$k_{nom} = (1 + k^*)(1 + I) - 1$$

Category	Calculation	% per annum
Sales	$(1.06)\,(1.10) - 1$	16.60
US components	$(1.06)\,(1.025) - 1$	8.65
Raw materials	$(1.06)\,(1.04) - 1$	10.24
Labor	$(1.06)\,(1.12) - 1$	18.72
G&A expense	$(1 + 0)\,(1.02) - 1$	2.00

The Fisher Effect is based on the fact that inflation is the loss of the purchasing power of money, that is, an increase in prices that is not associated with any increase in quality or quantity of goods. Inflation should be analyzed as part of the nominal required rate of return, where the nominal rate is the rate which is quoted or stated in contractual terms. The excess of the nominal rate of return over inflation is the real rate of return – the increase in volume in this case.

The real rate, k^*, and the nominal rate, k_{nom}, are connected by the rate of inflation. The nominal rate includes both the real rate and the inflation rate. This is referred to as the Fisher Effect. In this case, the application of the Fisher Effect suggests that sales increases should be anticipated at the rate of 16.6 percent per year. At the same time, US components will have a generally lower level of price increases that would suggest an 8.65 percent increase per year in these cash flows. Likewise, raw materials and labor will increase at the rates of 10.24 percent and 18.72 percent, respectively. General and administrative expense will increase at a 2 percent rate per year.

Identification of volume changes and differential inflation rates facilitates a line-by-line analysis of the Hsu Electronics acquisition.

Affiliate Cash Flows

Revenues, Expenses, and Dividends

Figure 6.7 outlines the sales, expenses, and dividends that are associated with the Hsu Electronics Company. Each line item represents one of the components of profitability for the enterprise. The first year's level of sales and expenses have been estimated based on the historical experience of Allied Electronics in the USA. The Chinese tax rate of 40 percent is used and the amount of dividends is based on the agreed upon dividend payout ratio of 50 percent. For years 2, 3, 4, and 5, each line item increases by the appropriate percentage as computed in Figure 6.6. Because sales increase faster than most elements of expense (labor cost is the only exception), net income is also projected to increase over time. Likewise, the dividend stream also increases because dividends are a constant percentage of net income. The dividend in the first year is estimated to be Rmb2.55 million. By year 5, the dividend is anticipated to have risen to Rmb9.6 million.

FIGURE 6.7

Hsu Electronics – Revenues, Expenses, and Dividends, Years 1 through 5

	Year				
	1	2	3	4	5
Sales	50,000	58,300	67,978	79,262	92,419
US components	(15,000)	(16,297)	(17,707)	(19,239)	(20,903)
Raw materials	(5,000)	(5,512)	(6,076)	(6,698)	(7,384)
Chinese labor	(9,500)	(11,278)	(13,389)	(15,895)	(18,871)
Gross margin	20,500	25,213	30,806	37,430	45,261
Licensing fee (1% of sales)	(500)	(583)	(680)	(793)	(924)
General and administrative expense	(10,000)	(10,200)	(10,404)	(10,612)	(10,824)
Depreciation	(1,500)	(1,500)	(1,500)	(1,500)	(1,500)
Earnings before interest and taxes	8,500	12,930	18,222	24,525	32,013
Taxes (@ 40%)	(3,400)	(5,172)	(7,289)	(9,810)	(12,805)
Net income	5,100	7,758	10,933	14,715	19,208
Dividends (50% of net income)	2,550	3,879	5,467	7,358	9,604

Notes:

Amounts are denominated in thousands of Renminbi.

See Figure 6.6 for rates of increase for specific line items.

FIGURE 6.8

Hsu Electronics – Working Capital Analysis Years 1 through 5

	Year				
	1	2	3	4	5
Sales	50,000	58,300	67,978	79,262	92,419
Year-end WC required[1]	12,500	14,575	16,995	19,816	23,105
Beginning of year WC balance	(10,000)[2]	(12,500)	(14,575)	(16,995)	(19,816)
WC change required	2,500	2,075	2,420	2,821	3,289

[1] Represents 25% of sales.
[2] Represents initial working capital investment.

Note: Amounts are in thousands of Renminbi.

Working Capital Changes

Figure 6.8 is an analysis of the working capital needs of Hsu Electronics. Recall that working capital requirements are estimated to be the same percentage of sales for Hsu Electronics as for the US parent, Allied Electronics, that is, working capital is 25 percent of sales. As sales will increase at the estimated rate of 16.6 percent per year (Figure 6.6), working capital will increase at the same rate. Allied Electronics will be required to invest Rmb10 million in the year of acquisition (time zero). As a result, only working capital increases in years 1, 2, 3, 4, and 5 need be considered in computing projected cash flows.[4] In the first year, an additional Rmb2.5 million will be required to support the level of sales. By year 5, the increase in working capital will have grown to Rmb3.3 million.

---

[4] Original levels of working capital are replenished when the cost of sales is recognized. That is, sales are reduced by cost of goods sold to arrive at gross margin. This reduction of gross proceeds implies that these funds are used to replace working capital. Thus, only *changes* in working capital need be considered when projecting cash flows of the acquisition.

FIGURE 6.9

Hsu Electronics – Projected After-tax Affiliate Cash Flows Years 0 through 5

				Year		
	0	1	2	3	4	5
Cost	(15,000)					
Sales revenue[1]		30,000	34,980	40,787	47,557	55,451
US component expense[1]		(9,000)	(9,778)	(10,624)	(11,543)	(12,542)
Raw materials expense[1]		(3,000)	(3,307)	(3,646)	(4,019)	(4,430)
Labor expense[1]		(5,700)	(6,767)	(8,033)	(9,537)	(11,323)
Licensing fee[1]		(300)	(350)	(408)	(476)	(554)
General and administrative expense[1]		(6,000)	(6,120)	(6,242)	(6,367)	(6,494)
Depreciation tax shield[2]		600	600	600	600	600
Working capital requirements[3]	(10,000)	(2,500)	(2,075)	(2,420)	(2,821)	(3,289)
Terminal value						20,000
Total	(25,000)	4,100	7,183	10,014	13,394	37,419

[1] Represents the amount shown in Figure 6.7, multiplied by $(1 - t)$, where $t = 0.40$.
[2] Represents the amount shown in Figure 6.7, multiplied by t, where $t = 0.40$.
[3] See Figure 6.8.

Note: Amounts are in thousands of Renminbi.

6

Projected Annual Cash Flows

Figure 6.9 summarizes the after-tax cash flows associated with Hsu Electronics. The negotiated price of the acquisition includes plant and equipment and working capital of Rmb25 million. Likewise, working capital increases are included as negative cash flows for years 1 through 5. A reversal of this working capital requirement and the sale of the facility are reflected in the negotiated sales price (terminal value) for the project at year 5 in the amount Rmb20 million.

During the five-year period, revenues and expenses in Figure 6.9 are reflected on an after-tax basis. Sales revenue, US components, raw materials, labor, licensing fees, and general and administrative expenses are based on information contained in Figure 6.7. As all of these components are either actual cash receipts or actual cash expenditures, they are adjusted to an after-tax amount by multiplying by $(1 - t)$.[5] The appropriate tax rate for these calculations is the Chinese tax rate of 40 percent.

The depreciation tax shield is a positive amount because depreciation expense during years 1–5 represents no outlay of cash but is, nevertheless, a tax-deductible item. At the Chinese tax rate of 40 percent, a deduction of depreciation in the amount of Rmb1.5 million produces a benefit of Rmb600,000, shown as a positive amount in Figure 6.9.

Analysis of Affiliate Cash Flows

The projected net cash flows for Hsu Electronics are an initial investment of Rmb25 million and positive cash flows for years 1–5 that range from Rmb4.1 million to Rmb37.4 million. These cash flows are the basis for the analysis of Hsu Electronics shown in Figure 6.10.

The payback period for the Hsu Electronics acquisition is 3.3 years. If Allied Electronics makes acquisitions that have a payback period of four years or more, Hsu Electronics is acceptable. For example, if the management of Allied Electronics has determined that any acquisition with a

---

[5] This means that 100 percent of the revenue is received but t percent is paid in taxes. In the case of cash expenses, 100 percent is paid, but – since these expenses are tax deductible – t percent is received as tax relief.

FIGURE 6.10

Hsu Electronics – Analysis of Projected Affiliate Cash Flows

Payback Period[1]	3.3 years
Internal Rate of Return	32.5%
Net Present Value[2]	Rmb10.697 million
Profitability Index	1.43[3]

[1] After year 3, Rmb3.703 million remains to be recovered. This is 28% of the net cash flow for year 4.
[2] Assumes a 20% cost of capital.
[3] The value of the acquisition at 20% is Rmb35.967 million. Since the cost of the acquisition is Rmb25 million, the profitability index is 1.43.

---

payback period of five years or less is acceptable, then Hsu Electronics clearly falls within this parameter.

The cost of capital is assumed to be 20 percent. This discount rate may be higher than that selected for domestic acquisitions of Allied, but the higher discount rate appears justified because of the higher level of political risk and the substantial foreign currency risk.

The internal rate of return is 32.5 percent. This compares favorably with the 20 percent minimum required rate of return and, again, suggests that the acquisition is acceptable.

The net present value at 20 percent discount is Rmb10.7 million. Thus, the value of this acquisition exceeds the price, also suggesting that it is a good value. The profitability index is a relatively high 1.43 indicating that for each Renminbi of investment Rmb1.43 is returned.

Within the PRC, Hsu Electronics is a viable acquisition. If acquired under the terms set forth, Hsu Electronics would add Rmb10.7 million to the wealth of a Chinese investor.

Parent Cash Flows

As the acquisition is being undertaken by Allied Electronics, a US company, it must also be analyzed from the perspective of a US investor.

FIGURE 6.11

Allied Electronics – Analysis of Dividends to be Received from Hsu Electronics

	Year				
	1	2	3	4	5
In Chinese Renminbi					
Dividends[1]	2,550	3,879	5,467	7,358	9,604
Pre-tax income required to pay dividends[2]	4,250	6,465	9,112	12,263	16,007
Tax on income at 40%[3]	1,700	2,586	3,645	4,905	6,403
In US Dollars					
Exchange rate ($/Rmb)[4]	0.161154	0.149911	0.139452	0.129723	0.120672
Pre-tax income required to pay dividends[5]	685	969	1,271	1,591	1,932
Tax on income at 34%[6]	(233)	(329)	(432)	(541)	(657)
Tax credit[7]	274	388	508	636	773
Net additional tax or tax credit[8]	41	59	76	95	116
Dividends received – gross[9]	411	582	762	955	1,159
Dividends received – net of tax[10]	452	641	838	1,050	1,275

[1] See Figure 6.7.
[2] AT = BT – tax
   = BT – BT(t)
   = BT$(1 - t)$
   AT$/(1 - t)$ = BT, where $t = 0.40$
[3] BT – AT = tax
   Pre-tax income – dividends = tax
[4] See Figure 6.3.
[5] [Exchange rate] × [Pre-tax income in Renminbi]
[6] [Pre-tax income in dollars] × [US tax rate]
[7] [Exchange rate] × [Tax paid in Renminbi]
[8] The net of US tax and Chinese tax credit.
[9] [Exchange rate] × [Dividends in Renminbi]
[10] [Net additional tax or tax credit] + [Dividends received – gross]

Note: Amounts are denominated in thousands of Renminbi or US dollars, as applicable.

Dividends

The dividends that will be received by Allied Electronics must be analyzed separately because they are paid in Renminbi on an after-tax basis. The taxes that are associated with these dividends in the PRC may be used as a tax credit in the USA. However, the amount of income that is included in Allied's US taxable income is not the amount of dividends. Instead, it is the amount of pre-tax income that was necessary to provide the after-tax payment of dividends. Figure 6.11 illustrates the calculation of the pre-tax income that is required to pay the dividends.

$$AT = BT - tax$$
$$AT = BT - BT(t)$$
$$AT = BT(1 - t)$$
$$\frac{AT}{(1 - t)} = BT$$

The above equation shows that, in order to arrive at the pre-tax income that is required to pay dividends, it is necessary to divide the after-tax dividend amount by $(1 - t)$. In year 1, the pre-tax income that is required to pay Rmb2.55 million is Rmb4.25 million.[6] Of course, the difference between the after-tax payment and the before-tax income is the amount of taxes. In year 1, taxes are Rmb1.7 million. Allied Electronics will include in taxable income the US equivalent of Rmb4.25 million and will receive a tax credit of the US equivalent of Rmb1.7 million.

The lower portion of Figure 6.11 shows the impact for Allied Electronics of these transactions in US dollars. First, the pre-tax income is translated from Renminbi to US dollars using the projected exchange rate for the applicable year.[7] In the case of year 1, each Renminbi is expected to be worth $0.161154. As a result, the US equivalent of the pre-tax income is

---

[6] This can be verified by noting that income of Rmb4.25 million implies income taxes of Rmb1.70 million (Rmb4.25 × 0.4), or an after-tax amount of Rmb2.55 million (Rmb4.25 million – Rmb1.70 million).

[7] See Figure 6.3.

$685,000. At a 34 percent tax rate, the tax liability in the USA is $233,000. There is a tax credit allowed, however, because of the taxes paid in the PRC. The US equivalent of the taxes paid in the PRC is $274,000. Accordingly, Allied Electronics receives a net tax credit of $41,000.

When the US equivalent of the gross amount of dividend income is computed, the result is $411,000. When this is added to the net tax credit of $41,000 in year 1, the dividends received by Allied Electronics (net-of-tax) amount to $452,000.

It should be noted that, if the tax rate in China had been lower than the rate in the USA, a net addition to tax would have resulted. In this case, the 40 percent tax rate in China is higher than the US tax rate, providing a net tax credit against other income earned by Allied Electronics elsewhere.

The remaining years 2–5 are analyzed in the same way. In each year, the net dividends increase. By the end of year 5, the US dollar equivalent of the dividends received by Allied from Hsu Electronics is $1.275 million. Having analyzed the dividend effect for Allied Electronics, it is now possible to include this information in an overall cash flow analysis of the Hsu Electronics project from the parent's perspective.

Cost of Acquisition

As shown in Figure 6.12, the cost of acquisition that will be required by Allied at the time of project initiation is Rmb25 million. At the current exchange rate, this translates to $4.331 million.

Licensing Fees and Component Profits

The licensing fees and gross profits on component exports to Hsu Electronics are received on a before-tax basis, translated directly into US dollars, and taxed. The difference between the treatment of these items and the treatment of dividends received is that dividends are received on an after-tax basis, that is, after Chinese taxes have been paid. In contrast, licensing fee and gross profits on component exports generate no tax

FIGURE 6.12

Allied Electronics – Parent Cash Flows Associated with Hsu Electronics

	Year					
	0	1	2	3	4	5
In Chinese Renminbi						
Cost of acquisition[1]	(25,000)					
Licensing fees[2]		500	583	680	793	924
Gross profit on components exports[3]		3,000	3,259	3,541	3,848	4,181
Project terminal value[4]						20,000
Subtotal	(25,000)	3,500	3,842	4,221	4,641	25,105
In US Dollars						
Exchange rate ($/Rmb)[5]	0.173241	0.161154	0.149911	0.139452	0.129723	0.120672
Taxable income[6]	–	564	576	589	602	616
Tax on income at 34%[7]	–	(192)	(196)	(200)	(205)	(209)
After-tax income[8]	–	372	380	389	397	407
Non-taxable cash flows[9]	(4,331)					2,413
After-tax dividends[10]	–	452	641	838	1,050	1,275
Total	(4,331)	824	1,021	1,227	1,447	4,095

[1] Non-deductible cash outflow for capital investment and working capital. See Figure 6.9.
[2] Taxable cash inflow. See Figure 6.7.
[3] Taxable cash inflow equal to 20% of cost for Hsu of US components. See Figure 6.7.
[4] Non-taxable cash inflow for sale of Hsu Electronics to Chinese investors. See Figure 6.9.
[5] See Figure 6.3.
[6] [Exchange rate] × [Licensing fee + gross profit on components]
[7] [Taxable income in dollars] × [US tax rate]
[8] Taxable income less tax.
[9] [Exchange rate] × [Project initial investment or terminal value]
[10] See Figure 6.11.

Note: Amounts are denominated in thousands of Renminbi or US dollars, as applicable.

liability for Hsu prior to payment to Allied because they are tax deductions. When licensing fees and gross profits on components are combined, the tax rate of 34 percent is applied to the US dollar equivalent. Again, each cash flow amount is subject only to the US tax rate of 34 percent.

Terminal Value

The terminal value of the project will be subject neither to Chinese nor to US tax. It is also translated into US dollars without any tax calculation.

When the after-tax amounts attributable to licensing fees and gross profits on component parts are added to the nontaxable cash flows of initial investment and terminal value, then added to the after-tax dividend amounts that are calculated in Figure 6.11, the result is the projected cash flows for Allied Electronics. The total cost of the acquisition is $4.331 million and will be paid in exchange for projected net cash flows in years 1–5 of $824,000, $1.021 million, $1.227 million, $1.447 million, and $4.095 million.

FIGURE 6.13

Allied Electronics – Analysis of Parent Cash Flows Associated with Hsu Electronics

Payback Period[1]	3.9 years
Internal Rate of Return	20.95%
Net Present Value[2]	$118,300
Profitability Index	1.03[3]

[1] After year 3, $1.259 million remains to be recovered. This is 87% of the net cash flow for year 4.
[2] Assumes a 20% cost of capital.
[3] The value of the project at 20% is $4.449 million. Since the initial investment is $4.331 million, the profitability index is 1.03.

Analysis of Parent Cash Flows

Figure 6.13 analyzes the cash flows to parent. The payback period for this acquisition is 3.9 years – roughly equivalent to the payback period computed from the perspective of a Chinese investor (3.3 years, see Figure 6.10). However, the internal rate of return (IRR) is considerably lower at 20.95 percent (versus 32.5 percent from the affiliate perspective). This is just marginally above the required return of 20 percent. Thus, it appears that the enterprise is decidedly more advantageous when viewed from the perspective of a Chinese investor than when analyzed from the perspective of a US investor.

The net present value (NPV) is positive, as would be expected since the IRR is greater than the minimum required rate of return. However, NPV is only marginally above zero at $118,300. On the other hand, the NPV from the perspective of the Chinese investor is a considerably higher at Rmb10.697 million.[8]

Likewise, the profitability index is greater than 1, but only marginally so. The 1.03 profitability index is considerably lower than the 1.43 profitability index for the project when it is analyzed from the perspective of a Chinese investor.

Renegotiating the Terms

These results suggest that this acquisition is indeed viable. However, from the viewpoint of Allied Electronics, there are less advantages than from the Chinese perspective. Allied has several options in attempting to renegotiate the terms of the investment with Chinese officials.

- A higher licensing fee for Allied Electronics would shift some of the profitability of the project from the Chinese operation to the US parent.
- A higher gross profit on component parts would accomplish the same objective.

---

[8] This is $1.29 million at the least favorable exchange rate given in Figure 6.3 (Rmb10.697 million × 0.120672 $/Rmb).

- The amount of dividends received by Allied Electronics could be increased to enhance the positive cash flow from the project.
- The terminal value could be increased.

The third alternative recognizes the direct link between the amount of dividends and the amount of net income. In this way, this alternative lowers the burden on the Chinese operation as dividends are paid after all operating expenses and taxes have been paid.

The fourth alternative essentially increases the amount of investment by Chinese investors to take over the profitable operation, transferring more of the future profitability of the project to Allied at the end of five years. The last alternative might be attractive to the Chinese government because it represents an even lighter burden on the enterprise than the first three alternatives during the early years. It also delays a large cash flow to Allied in compensation for its technology transfer.

SUMMARY OF ISSUES SURROUNDING A MULTINATIONAL ACQUISITION

The acquisition of a multinational company involves the risks of fluctuating exchange rates and political risk. In this case, the length of time that Allied is permitted to invest in the Chinese company is limited by the government of that country. The dividends that may be repatriated are negotiated with the host country. The exchange rate itself changes over time and affects the dollar value of income to the US parent company. As the Renminbi declines in value, dollar proceeds to the parent company also decline.

One of the most crucial elements of a multinational acquisition is the distinction between affiliate cash flows and parent cash flows. In many cases, the acquisition will be viable and profitable from the perspective of the host country. However, when evaluated from the perspective of the foreign investor, the potential acquisition may be less attractive. Because of this potential difference, it is critical to analyze all aspects of a multinational acquisition from the perspectives of both the host country and parent country investors.

6

APPENDIX A

THE TIME VALUE OF MONEY

INTRODUCTION

The cash flows that are used to determine value in mergers and acquisitions are evaluated over long periods of time. This process necessitates consideration of the time value of money. This appendix outlines the concepts and illustrates the application of the time value of money.

INDIVIDUAL CASH FLOWS

The concept of the time value of money can be capsulized in one statement:

A dollar received today is worth more than a dollar received one year from today.

Expanding this logic, a given cash flow can be valued at any point in time. From a conceptual standpoint, the passage of time may be depicted by a time line. A time line begins with the current period – the current point in time – and identifies other points in time that are exactly one, two, three, four, or more years in the future. Each point on the time line indicates a specific moment. The space between these points indicates the passage of time.

Future Value

Figure A.1 illustrates both the time line and a specific cash flow. In this example, $100 is valued as of today, that is, time zero. A question that would correspond with this time line is, "If you deposited $100 in an account that paid 8 percent and then left the account untouched for five years, to what amount would the balance have grown at the end of five years?"

The answer is actually a series of steps. The first step is to determine the value of the deposit at the end of one year. The reason for this first step is that 8 percent is an annual interest rate, thus it is necessary to determine the balance in the account at the end of the first year. This is equivalent

---

FIGURE A.1

The Future Value of a Single Amount

0	1	2	3	4	5
					$*$
100.00					?

FV_1	$=$	100.00 (1.08)	$=$	108.00
FV_2	$=$	108.00 (1.08)	$=$	116.64
FV_3	$=$	116.64 (1.08)	$=$	125.97
FV_4	$=$	125.97 (1.08)	$=$	136.05
FV_5	$=$	136.05 (1.08)	$=$	146.93

or

FV_5	$=$	$100.00 (1.08)^5$	$=$	146.93

Future Value Interest Factor:

$$FVIF_{k,n} = (1 + k)^n$$
$$FVIF_{0.08,5} = (1.08)^5 = 1.469328$$

Future Value of a Single Amount:

$$FV_n = PV (1 + k)^n$$
$$= PV (FVIF_{k,n})$$

---

to asking the question "What is the future value of $100 placed in an 8 percent account for one year?" The answer is $108 as shown in Figure A.1. That is, FV_1, the future value of $100 at the end of period 1, equals PV, present value of $100, multiplied by (1.08).

This process is repeated in year 2. The value at the end of year 2, that is, FV_2, equals $116.64. This is, of course, $108 multiplied by (1.08). This process continues for the next three years so that the future value at the end of period 5, that is, FV_5, is $146.93.

In other words, the future value at year 5, FV_5, equals $100 multiplied by $(1.08)^5$. The $100 original principal or PV is multiplied by the quantity (1.08) a total of five times. This relationship is standardized in the sense that the amount of interest and principle $(1 + k)$ has been identified as a specific multiplicative factor called future value interest factor, abbreviated as $FVIF_{k,n}$. The future value interest factor is identified as $(1 + k)^n$. As also indicated in Figure A.1, the future value interest factor for the combination of 8 percent and five years is $(1.08)^5$, or 1.469328.

When time value of money principles are generalized, the future value of a single amount can be specified by a relationship shown in Figure A.1. The future value of a single amount at any point on the time line may be found by multiplying the present value by the relevant FVIF. This relationship will always hold true and can be used in any case. The FVIF is a function of two variables – the rate of interest for the year and the number of years that are involved.

The valuation formula for the future value of a single amount is:

$$FV_n = PV\,(1 + k)^n = PV\,(FVIF_{k,n}) \tag{1}$$

Present Value

The example in the above section answers the question of how much an amount will grow to after five years if placed on deposit at a rate of 8 percent. It is also possible to use time value of money concepts to determine the amount one would be willing to pay today for a future payment, as shown in Figure A.2.

Assume now that the question is, "How much would you be willing to pay today in exchange for the right to receive a cash flow of $200 at the end of five years if you required 8 percent on your investment?" This question is equivalent to, "What is the present value of $200 at 8 percent for five years?" This situation still involves a single amount and the basic equation for the future value of a single amount. The difference is that the future value is known and the present value is not. As above, the rate of interest and the number of years are given. In this case, the present value equals the future value multiplied by the inverse of $(1 + k)^5$. Substituting $200 for the future value, 8 percent for k, and 5 for n, the present value is $136.12. In other words, an individual whose required rate of return is 8 percent would pay $136.12 in exchange for the right to receive $200 at the end of year 5.

FIGURE A.2

Present Value of a Single Amount

0	1	2	3	4	5
*					
?					200

$$FV_s = PV\,(1 + k)^5$$

$$PV\,(1 + k)^5 = FV_s$$

$$PV = FV_s\left(\frac{1}{(1 + k)^5}\right)$$

Substituting,

$$PV = 200\left(\frac{1}{(1.08)^5}\right)$$

$$= 136.12$$

Present Value Interest Factor:

$$PVIF_{n,k} = \left(\frac{1}{(1 + k)^n}\right)$$

Present Value of a Single Amount:

$$PV = FV_n\left(\frac{1}{(1 + k)^n}\right)$$

$$= FV_n\,(PVIF_{k,n})$$

$$FV_n = PV(1 + k)^n = PV(FVIF_{k,n})$$

As was true with the future value problem, a standardized factor can be derived to determine the present value. This factor is called the present value interest factor. It is calculated as the inverse of $(1 + k)^5$. In this case, the PVIF is 0.680583.

In general, the future value equation is used to solve for the present value. Solving for present value means isolating present value on one side of the equal sign and placing all other terms on the other side of the equal sign.

The valuation formula for the present value of a single amount is:

$$PV = FV_n \left(\frac{1}{(1 + k)^n} \right) = FV_n(PVIF_{k,n}) \tag{2}$$

Implied Rate of Return

Up to this point, the formula in Figure A.1 has been used to find the future value and the present value of a single amount. It is also possible

---

FIGURE A.3

Implied Rate of Return

0	1	2	3	4	5
*					
(400)					674.02

$$FV_5 = PV (1 + k)^5$$
$$PV (1 + k)^5 = FV_5$$
$$(1 + k)^5 = (FV_5/PV)$$

Taking the fifth root of both sides,
$$(1 + k) = (FV_5/PV)^{1/5}$$
$$k = (FV_5/PV)^{1/5} - 1$$

Substituting,
$$k = (674.02/400)^{1/5} - 1$$
$$= (1.68505)^{1/5} - 1$$
$$= 0.10999$$
$$= 0.11$$

Implied Rate of Return:
$$FV_n = PV(1 + k)^n$$
$$k = (FV_n/PV)^{1/n} - 1$$

---

to use the same formula and solve for k. The relevant question in this case is, "What rate of return does an investor receive if the investor pays a specified price today in exchange for a promised payoff in the future?" Figure A.3 presents an example. The question that can be associated with this time line is, "If an investor paid $400 for the right to receive $674.02 in five years, what rate of return would that investor expect on average each year?" The answer is the rate implied by the single-amount formula, with PV = $400, FV_s = $674.02, and $n = 5$.

Dividing both sides of the single-amount equation by PV, leaves $(1 + k)^5$. To solve for k, it is necessary to take the fifth root of both sides of the equation. In this way, the quantity $(1 + k)$ is isolated on the left-hand side of the equation.[1] When 1 is subtracted from both sides, the result is that the implied rate of return, or k, is $(FV_s/PV)^{1/5} - 1$. Substituting the values that are relevant here and solving for k, the implied rate of return is 11 percent. When this relationship is generalized, it is clear that the implied rate of return is a function of the future value, the present value, and the number of periods that elapse between them.

The formula for implied rate of return in the case of a single amount is:

$$k = \left(\frac{FV_n}{PV} \right)^{1/n} - 1 \tag{3}$$

Notice that one equation has been used to satisfy three requirements. All of the problems have been solved using the formula for the future value of a single amount, varying only the unknown. In Figure A.1, the

---

[1] Whenever a quantity that already has been raised to a power (other than 1) is raised to another power, the powers or exponents are multiplied in order to arrive at the value of the quantity. In this case, raising both sides of the equation to the 1/5 power, or taking the fifth root, results in the left-hand side being raised to the power of 1.

unknown was future value, in Figure A.2 present value, and in Figure A.3 implied rate of return.

Implied Rate of Return versus Required Rate of Return

In the examples above, two concepts of rate of return were employed. The first was a required rate of return, when k was specified as 8 percent in Figures A.1 and A.2. In both cases, 8 percent was given. The rate was a function of some external decision with respect to the appropriate rate of return. On the other hand, k was the unknown in Figure A.3. The differentiation is between required rate of return and expected rate of return.

Looking at it another way, Figure A.2 is an exercise that answers the question, "What is the present value of a single amount?" This question can be restated as, "What is the maximum that an investor should be willing to pay today in order to receive $200 at the end of five years if 8 percent was the investor's minimum required rate of return?" In both Figures A.1 and A.2, the external decision making with respect to the rate of return was completed beforehand. In an actual case, the rate of return is an extremely important factor that must be determined by the decision maker on the basis of the current interest rate environment and the risk involved in the project.

The first two cases are contrasted with the third case in which the rate of return is the unknown. In Figure A.3, the question is, "What rate of return would an investor earn on average each year if the investor paid $400 today with the promise of receiving $674.02 in five years?" This rate of return is derived from given cash flows. It is not necessary to determine the risk of the project. In fact, the risk of the project is irrelevant to the calculation. This rate of return is a mathematical result – simply the rate that will cause the present value of $674.02 to equal $400 or the expected return.

The required rate of return must be based on some objective criterion and the expected rate of return will always be a function of the cash flows that are given.

Point of Valuation

Implicit in the discussions thus far has been the concept of point of valuation. As noted above, the time line identifies points in time that occur one, two, three, four, or five years after today – time zero. Recall also that any cash flow may be valued anywhere along the time line. In the cases that we have used up to this point, the cash flow occurred either at time zero (future value calculation), time 5 (present value calculation), or both (implied rate of return).

Referring to Figure A.1, recall that the cash flow itself occurred at time zero but the question was, "What is the value of that cash flow at time 5?" In this case, the point of valuation, or the point on the time line at which the $100 was to be valued, was year 5.

Looking again at Figure A.2, the cash flow of $200 occurred at time 5. The question was, "How much would an investor be willing to pay today, time zero?" In this example, time zero was a point of valuation.

The point of valuation for a single amount is the point on the time line at which a cash flow is valued.

The interpretation of *n* in this exercise is the number of periods between the cash flow and the point of valuation. This point of valuation may occur anywhere along the time line.

INTRA-YEAR COMPOUNDING

Up to this point, all compounding has been on an annual basis, that is, interest has been computed only one time per year. Intra-year compounding involves compounding more than one time during the year. Figure A.4 is essentially the same case as in Figure A.1, with one exception. Instead of 8 percent being paid each year, 4 percent is paid each six-month period.

As shown in Figure A.4, at the end of the first six months, the balance will have grown to $104. By the end of year 1, the balance is not $108 in Figure A.1, but is instead $108.16. Each successive six-month period results in the compounding, or growth, of the balance at the rate of 4 percent. At the end of five years – again, the point of valuation is year 5 – the value of the account is $148.02.

Recall that with annual compounding (Figure A.1) over an equivalent five-year period at 8 percent, $100 grew to $146.93. The difference between these two amounts – $1.09 – is interest on interest. Effectively,

---

FIGURE A.4

Intra-year Compounding – Future Value – Semi-annual Case

0	1	2	3	4	5
					*
100					?

$FV_{0.5}$	=	100.00 (1.04)	=	104.00
FV_1	=	104.00 (1.04)	=	108.16
$FV_{1.5}$	=	108.16 (1.04)	=	112.49
FV_2	=	112.49 (1.04)	=	116.99
$FV_{2.5}$	=	116.99 (1.04)	=	121.67
FV_3	=	121.67 (1.04)	=	126.54
$FV_{3.5}$	=	126.54 (1.04)	=	131.60
FV_4	=	131.60 (1.04)	=	136.86
$FV_{4.5}$	=	136.86 (1.04)	=	142.33
FV_5	=	142.33 (1.04)	=	148.02

---

interest is earned earlier, is added to the balance, and begins earning interest sooner. It should be noted that interest on interest is also earned in the annual case, but that in the intra-year compounding case, the interest on interest accrues faster.

There are three new concepts that are applied when intra-year compounding is introduced.

- The number of times per year interest is paid or compounded is denoted by m. In the case of semi-annual compounding, or compounding twice a year, the value of m is 2.
- The rate of return per period is also relevant. In the previous examples (Figures A.1 through A.3), the rate of return was stated as an annual rate. While rates are always quoted on an annual basis, even in an intra-year compounding case, the rate must be adjusted to the rate per period for the purposes of time value of money concepts. This adjustment is made by dividing k by m to arrive at the rate per period.
- The number of periods must be substituted for the number of years. For the previous example, the number of periods equaled the number of years. When intra-year compounding is used, this is not the case. The number of periods will be the number of years multiplied by the number of periods per year.

Figure A.5 shows the impact of intra-year compounding using the present value of $100 and an annual rate of 8 percent over a five-year period. The first two entries, annual and semi-annual, were computed above and are presented for comparative purposes.

Essentially when annual compounding applies and the rate of interest is 8 percent annually over five years, the future value interest factor is 1.469328 or $(1.08)^5$. In the case of semi-annual compounding, the factor is adjusted so that 4 percent is the rate per period and the number of periods is ten, that is, the factor is computed as $(1.04)^{10}$. The result is that $100 grows to $148.02 rather than $146.93. When compounding frequency increases to four times per year – that is, quarterly – the rate of return per period decreases to 2 percent but the number of periods

FIGURE A.5

Intra-year Compounding – Varying Intervals

Given: PV   =   100.00

              annual rate   =   0.08

              number of years =   5

Compounding Frequency	m	$FVIF_{k,n}$	FV_5
Annual	1	$(1.08)^5 = 1.469328$	146.93
Semi-annual	2	$(1.04)^{10} = 1.480244$	148.02
Quarterly	4	$(1.02)^{20} = 1.485947$	148.59
Monthly	12	$(1.006667)^{60} = 1.489875$	148.99
Daily	365	$(1.000219)^{1825} = 1.491275$	149.13

m = number of times per year interest is compounded or paid

k = annual rate/m

   = rate per period

n = (m)(number of years)

   = number of periods

increases to 20. The result is that the future value is $148.59. On a monthly basis, the rate of return decreases to 0.6667 percent per period and the number of periods increases to 60. The future value then is $148.99. When the compounding frequency increases to daily, there are 365 compounding periods per year. Over a five-year period, this results in 1,825 periods but the rate per period is substantially smaller at 0.0219 percent per period. Accordingly, the future value increases to $149.13.

When computing future value, intra-year compounding causes the results to increase as the number of periods per year increases. Conversely, the more frequent the intra-year compounding, the smaller will be the results of present value calculations.

CONTINUOUS COMPOUNDING

The intra-year compounding that was discussed in the previous section, regardless of the frequency, is still considered discreet compounding. Discreet compounding means that the periods of time are measured with a beginning and ending point in time, even if the beginning and ending points are extremely close together.

On the other hand, when it is not possible to differentiate the beginning and ending of a compounding period, the method of compounding is said to be continuous. With continuous compounding, the interval over which interest is compounded is infinitely small. This compounding method requires a different form of the valuation formula for a single amount.

$$FV_n = PV \ (e^{kt}) \tag{4}$$

FIGURE A.6
Continuous Compounding – Future Value

$$
\begin{array}{cccccc}
0 & 1 & 2 & 3 & 4 & 5 \\
 & & & & & * \\
100 & & & & & ?
\end{array}
$$

$$FV_n \ = \ PV(e^{kt})$$

Substituting,

$$
\begin{aligned}
FV_5 \ &= \ 100 \ (e^{(0.08)(5)}) \\
&= \ 100 \ (e^{0.40}) \\
&= \ 100 \ (1.491825) \\
&= \ 149.18
\end{aligned}
$$

Future Value

The formula and its application are illustrated in Figure A.6, using the example of a $100 deposit at 8 percent for five years. The question once again is, "What is the future value of the $100 at 8 percent?" But because it is impossible to identify specific periods and the rate per period (because of the shortness of the compounding intervals), the future value must be respecified. The future value at period n equals the present value multiplied by e^{kt}, where e is the natural logarithm function with the value of 2.718281828, k is the appropriate annual rate, and t is the number of years that apply. In most cases, this function will be included on a financial or scientific calculator as the key e^x. It is not possible to perform this continuous compounding equation without either using a preprogrammed calculator key, e^x, or the base equivalent of 2.718281828.

Although the example in Figure A.6 may be done either way, the preprogrammed calculator approach is demonstrated. Substituting $100 for present value, 0.08 for k, and 5 for t, $100 \times e^{0.40} = 100 \times 1.491825$. The result is that the future value at 5 is $149.18. This is the highest future value that can be obtained at 8 percent over five years. Notice that it is even greater than the daily compounding result by 5 cents. Thus, the range of values for the future value of $100 at 8 percent over five years is from $146.93 to $149.18. This range directly relates to the frequency of compounding – from annual compounding to continuous compounding. All other compounding frequencies will yield results that fall within this range.

Present Value

Figure A.7 illustrates the use of continuous compounding to find present values. As was the case with the example in Figure A.2, the question is, "What is the maximum that an investor would be willing to pay today in order to receive $200 in five years if the minimum required rate of return was 8 percent?" In this case, the question is qualified by stipulating continuous compounding. The future value formula using continuous

		FIGURE A.7		

Continuous Compounding – Present Value

0	1	2	3	4	5
*					
?					200

$$FV_n = PV(e^{kt})$$

$$PV(e^{kt}) = FV_n$$

$$PV = FV_n \left(\frac{1}{e^{kt}} \right)$$

Substituting,

$$PV = 200 \left(\frac{1}{e^{(0.08)(5)}} \right)$$

$$= 200 \left(\frac{1}{1.4918247} \right)$$

$$= 200(0.670320)$$

$$= 134.06$$

compounding is used to solve for present value. That is, present value is isolated on the left-hand side of the equation while all other terms are isolated on the other side of the equation.

$$PV = FV_n \left(\frac{1}{e^{kt}} \right) \tag{5}$$

Substituting the specific values in this problem, present value equals $200 multiplied by 0.670320 or $134.06. Notice that the difference between the results of Figure A.7 and the results of Figure A.2 is $2.06 (136.12 – 134.06). When continuous compounding is applied, it is necessary to invest $2.06 less to obtain a $200 payoff in year 5 as compared to annual compounding.

Implied Rate of Return

Figure A.8 illustrates the application of the implied rate of return using continuous compounding. The example is parallel to that in Figure A.3, that is, a $400 payment in exchange for $674.02 to be received in five years. The equation is the same as that used in Figures A.6 and A.7, FV = PV(e^{kt}). The difference between this approach and that used in Figure A.3 is the way in which k is determined. The equation again must be solved so that k is isolated on one side of the equation while all other terms are isolated on the other side.

Now k is a part of the exponent of base e. It is necessary to find the natural log of FV_n/PV and then solve for k. It is necessary at this point to use a natural log key, often indicated as LN on financial calculators. Unlike the future value and present value cases, in which it is possible to

---

FIGURE A.8

Continuous Compounding – Implied Rate of Return

0	1	2	3	4	5
*					
(400)					674.02

$$FV_n = PV(e^{kt})$$
$$PV(e^{kt}) = FV_n$$
$$e^{kt} = FV_n/PV$$
$$k = \ln(FV_n/PV)/t$$

where $\quad \ln(FV_n/PV)$ = natural log of FV_n/PV
$$= kt$$

Substituting,
$$e^{kt} = 674.02/400$$
$$= 1.685050$$

$$\ln(1.685050) = 0.521795$$
$$= k(5)$$
$$k = 0.521795/5$$
$$= 0.104359$$

---

arrive at the solution using the numerical value of e, it is not possible to identify the implied rate of return in any way other than using the natural log (LN) function of a calculator.

The process is to enter the ratio of future value to present value and activate the natural log key. When this is done, the result is the specific exponent of e (kt) that will cause e^{kt} to equal the ratio of FV_n/PV. This exponent (the log of the ratio of future value to present value) then actually represents the product of the rate of return and the number of years. Notice in this case that the rate of return will be the annual rate and that t is the number of years. The concept of number of periods within a year has no meaning in continuous compounding because the intervals are infinitely small. Thus, all periods are stated in number of years and all rates are stated on an annual basis.

Substituting the values that apply in this example, we find that e^{kt} equals 1.685050. First entering this value and then finding its natural log results in a value of 0.521795. This number is interpreted as k multiplied by five (the number of years). In other words, it is five times the annual rate of return. Dividing this number by five yields the annual rate of 0.104359 or 10.44 percent.

Comparing this result to the result in Figure A.3 illustrates the impact of using continuous compounding or intra-year compounding versus annual compounding. In the case of continuous compounding, the expected annual rate of return is 10.44 percent. In the case of annual compounding the expected return is 11.00 percent. This is interpreted to mean that, on a continuous basis, the rate of return that is required to cause $400 to grow to $674.02 is lower than the rate of return that is necessary when that amount is compounded on an annual basis. This generally will be the case – a lower rate of return will achieve the same results when continuous compounding is used vis-à-vis annual compounding.

GENERAL CONCEPTS

The same logic extends generally to intra-year compounding, as well. Whenever intra-year compounding is used and the results compared with annual compounding, certain general results can be expected.

- When the future value is computed using intra-year or continuous compounding, the result will be greater than the future value found using annual compounding.
- When intra-year or continuous compounding is used to find the present value of a single amount, the present value will be lower or smaller than the result that will be obtained when annual compounding is used.
- In finding the expected rate of return when intra-year or continuous compounding is used, the rate will be lower than that obtained when the calculation assumes annual compounding.

In each case, a basic formula will apply. In the case of discreet compounding that formula is the future value interest factor of a single amount. It is the formula that is contained in Figure A.1:

$$FV_n = PV\,(1 + k)^n$$

This formula can be manipulated or changed depending upon the variable that is unknown. It can be used to find future value, present value, or implied rate of return.

In the case of continuous compounding, the basic equation is contained in Figure A.6:

$$FV_n = PVe^{kt}$$

This equation can be used to find future value, present value and implied or expected rate of return.

ANNUITIES

Up to this point, only single amounts have been valued at various points along the time line. Time value of money concepts may also be applied to multiple cash flows. Annuities, defined in Figure A.9, are an important subset of multiple cash flows. As long as cash flows meet these criteria, those cash flows constitute an annuity. This set of criteria stipulates that the cash flows must be equal in amount, with equal intervals between them, and that there must be a finite number of cash flows. When these conditions are met, there are certain concepts that make the process of finding the value of these multiple cash flows more efficient.

FIGURE A.9

Defining an Annuity

As long as the following conditions are met, a set of multiple cash flows constitutes an annuity:

■ a series of cash flows

■ cash flows of equal amount

■ equal intervals between cash flows

■ a finite number of cash flows.

Future Value

Figure A.10 is an example of an annuity with five cash flows, each in the amount of $100. Because each cash flow is identical, the cash flows are identified as specific cash flows that apply to a specific year. For example, CF_1 is the cash flow in year 1. The first example of an annuity asks the question, "What would be the balance in an account in which $100 is invested in each of the next five years, beginning one year from now, if the account earns 8 percent, compounded annually?" The point of valuation is assumed to be immediately after the last deposit is made. In essence, the point of valuation can be assumed to coincide with the last cash flow but would include valuation of the fifth cash flow.

FIGURE A.10

Future Value of an Annuity

0	1	2	3	4	5
					*
	100	100	100	100	100
	CF_1	CF_2	CF_3	CF_4	CF_5
					?

$$
\begin{aligned}
FV &= CF_1(1.08)^4 + CF_2(1.08)^3 + CF_3(1.08)^2 + CF_4(1.08)^1 + CF_5(1.08)^0 \\
&= 100[(1.08)^4 + (1.08)^3 + (1.08)^2 + (1.08)^1 + (1.08)^0] \\
&= 100\ [1.360489 + 1.259712 + 1.1664 + 1.08 + 1] \\
&= 100\ [5.866601] \\
&= 586.66
\end{aligned}
$$

$$
FV_n = CF\ \left(\sum_{t=1}^{n} (1 + k)^t \right)
$$

$$
= CF(FVIFA_{k,n})
$$

$$
\text{where } FVIFA_{k,n} = [(1 + k)^n - 1]/k
$$

The value of the annuity is the sum of the values of the individual cash flows. Thus, the problem may be restated as one in which it is necessary to find the future value of each of the five individual payments. The future value of the first cash flow, CF_1, is determined by compounding this amount for four periods. Four periods is the appropriate number of periods for CF_1 because four years elapse between the point of valuation (year 5) and the cash flow (year 1). Likewise, the appropriate number of periods to compound CF_2 is three because three years elapse between the cash flow (year 2) and the point of valuation (year 5). Using the same logic, each successive cash flow is compounded for one less period.

When $100 is substituted for each of the cash flows, that constant value may be factored out of each term on the right-hand side of the equation. What remains within the brackets on the right-hand side of the equation is a series of terms, each equal to (1.08) raised to the appropriate power. Notice that the last factor is raised to the power of zero. This is because the cash flow is received and immediately valued. Since no time passes between the time of the cash flow and the time of valuation, there is no increase in the value of CF_5 and it is worth $100.

What is left in the bracket is the sum of individual future value interest factors, or FVIFs, equal to 5.866601. Multiplying this factor by $100, the future value of this annuity is $586.66. The answer to the question shows that the five $100 cash flows will be worth more than $500 in principal because the first four cash flows compound and earn interest, although the last cash flow does not.

This example can be generalized into the future value of an annuity, where the future value is the cash flow multiplied by the sum of the relevant single amount factors. This sum of relevant single amount future value interest factors has also been standardized into a factor called the future value interest factor of an annuity, $FVIFA_{k,n}$. In addition, the sum of the single amount factors, or $FVIFA_{k,n}$, converges to the closed-form equation in Figure A.10:

$$FVIFA_{k,n} = \left(\frac{(1 + k)^n - 1}{k} \right) \tag{6}$$

Present Value

The approach for finding the present value of the same annuity is illustrated in Figure A.11. In this case, the question might be, "What is the maximum amount that an investor would be willing to pay today to receive five annual $100 payments, with the first occurring one year from today, if 8 percent is the investor's minimum required rate of return?" This requires finding the present value of each of the individual cash flows. In this case, CF_1 is discounted at 8 percent for one period because there is one period between the point of valuation (year 0) and the cash flow (year 1).

FIGURE A.11

Present Value of an Annuity

0	1	2	3	4	5
*					
	100	100	100	100	100
	CF_1	CF_2	CF_3	CF_4	CF_5
?					

$$PV = CF_1 \left(\frac{1}{1.08}\right) + CF_2 \left(\frac{1}{(1.08)^2}\right) + CF_3 \left(\frac{1}{(1.08)^3}\right) + CF_4 \left(\frac{1}{(1.08)^4}\right) + CF_5 \left(\frac{1}{(1.08)^5}\right)$$

$$= 100 \left[\frac{1}{(1.08)} + \frac{1}{(1.08)^2} + \frac{1}{(1.08)^3} + \frac{1}{(1.08)^4} + \frac{1}{(1.08)^5}\right]$$

$$= 100 \left[0.925926 + 0.857339 + 0.793832 + 0.735030 + 0.670583\right]$$
$$= 100 \left[3.99271\right]$$
$$= 399.27$$

$$PV = CF \left(\sum_{t=1}^{n} \frac{1}{(1+k)^t}\right)$$

$$= CF(PVIFA_{k,n})$$

where $PVIFA_{k,n} = 1 - [1/(1+k)^n]/k$

Cash flow 2 is discounted for two years because there are two periods between the point of valuation (year 0) and the cash flow (year 2). Each successive cash flow is discounted for one more year.

As was true in the previous example, $100 is substituted and then factored out of each term on the right-hand side of the equation. This leaves within the brackets the individual single amount present value factors using 8 percent for years 1–5. The sum of these factors is 3.99271 and the value of the annuity is $399.27.

The generalized formula for the present value of an annuity is CF multiplied by the sum of the relevant PVIFs or CF multiplied by $PVIFA_{k,n}$. $PVIFA_{k,n}$ also converges to a closed form equation:

$$PVIFA_{k,n} = \left(\frac{1 - \dfrac{1}{(1 + k)^n}}{k} \right) \qquad (7)$$

INTERPRETING FACTORS

There are implied points of valuation built into the annuity factors and into the financial functions of hand-held calculators and spreadsheet programs. The implied points of valuation must be understood in order to apply the factors correctly or use the built-in functions properly.

In the case of the future value interest factor of an annuity, the factor yields a value for the annuity that is valid only for the point on the time line that coincides exactly with last cash flow.

In other words, if year 5 had not been the point of valuation according to the stated problem, then it would not have been possible to sum the individual factors to arrive at the closed-form annuity factor that is defined in Figure A.10 and Equation 6.

Likewise, in Figure A.11, if the point of valuation of the problem had not been year 0, that is, one year prior to CF_1, it would not have been possible to arrive at the exact annuity factor that corresponds with the closed-form factor in Figure A.11 and Equation 7.

In the case of the present value interest factor of an annuity, the factor yields a value for the annuity that is valid only for the point on the time line that is one period before the first cash flow.

$FVIFA_{k,n}$ assumes a point of valuation that corresponds with the last cash flow. $PVIFA_{k,n}$ assumes a point of valuation that is one period before the first cash flow.

The number of periods is different in analyzing annuity factors versus single amount factors. The interpretation of n *in a single amount factor*, as noted earlier, is the *number of periods that elapse between the cash flow and the point of valuation*. In the case of an annuity, this definition has little meaning because there is one implied point of valuation but multiple cash flows. The proper interpretation of n *for an annuity factor is the number of cash flows in the annuity*. This means that application of the annuity factor for a five-year annuity will yield the same value regardless of which five years are involved.

Figure A.12 summarizes the important concepts to remember when

FIGURE A.12		
Interpreting Factors		
	Interpretation for	
Variable	**Single amount**	**Annuity**
n	Number of periods between POV and CF	Number of CFs
Implied POV	None	For FVIFA, coincides with last CF
		For PVIFA, one period before first CF

Notes:
CF means cash flow
POV means point of valuation

applying single amount and annuity factors. For a single amount factor, there is no implied point of valuation. There is only a point of valuation according to the specific scenario. For example, a cash flow of $100 may be valued anywhere along the time line. The determination of n will depend entirely on the specific situation.

On the other hand, in the case of annuities, there is an implied point of valuation for both future value and present value factors. For the future value interest factor of an annuity, the implied point of valuation coincides exactly with the last cash flow in the annuity. For the present value interest factor of an annuity, the point of valuation is one period before the first cash flow in the annuity. In the event that the actual point of valuation that is stipulated by the specific scenario does not match the implied point of valuation, certain adjustments must be made.

FIGURE A.13

Example for Interpreting Future Value Annuity Factors

0	1	2	3	4	5	6	7	8
								★
	100	100	100	100	100			
								?

$$FV_5 = 100[FVIFA_{0.08,5}]$$
$$= 100[(1.08)^5 - 1)/0.08]$$
$$= 100[5.866601]$$
$$= 586.66$$

$$FV_8 = FV_5[FVIF_{0.08,3}]$$
$$= 586.66 [(1.08)^3]$$
$$= 586.66 [1.259712]$$
$$= 739.02$$

Figure A.13 is an example of the case in which the implied point of valuation for a factor differs from the point of valuation stipulated by a specific scenario. Once again, this is a five-year annuity of $100 that begins one year from today. However, in this case, the question is, "How much is this annuity worth at the end of year 8?" A possible scenario

---

associated with this time line might be a series of payments into an investment vehicle for retirement – through year 5 – but the inability to withdraw any of the funds without tax penalty until year 8.

It is still possible to use the future value interest factor of an annuity, but it is also necessary to adjust the FVIFA result. When FVIFA for a five-year annuity at 8 percent is multiplied by $100, the result is once again $586.66, a value that is correct as of the end of year 5 (see also Figure A.10). But if the funds are not to be used until year 8, they will be allowed to continue to compound for the next three years. The question is not how much the annuity it worth at the end of year 5, but rather how much it will be worth at the end of year 8?

At the end of year 5, the annuity is equivalent to the single amount of $586.66. Multiplying this amount by the FVIF for 8 percent and three years, yields the final result of $739.02. Three years is used for the single amount factor FVIF because the annuity has been reduced to $586.66 as of year 5.[2] Since the point of valuation according to the scenario is year 8, the difference of three years requires use of $n = 3$.

FIGURE A.14

Example for Interpreting Present Value Annuity Factors

0	1	2	3	4	5	6	7	8	9	10
		*				100	100	100	100	100
		?								

$$PV_5 = 100[PVIFA_{0.08,5}]$$
$$= 100[(1 - 1/(1.08)^5)/0.08]$$
$$= 100[3.99271]$$
$$= 399.27$$

$$PV_2 = 399.27 [PVIF_{0.08,3}]$$
$$= 399.27 [1/(1.08)^3]$$
$$= 399.27 [0.793832]$$
$$= 316.95$$

[2] An investor with a required return of 8 percent would be indifferent between (1) receiving the five-year annuity and (2) receiving $586.66 at the end of year 5.

Likewise, a present value annuity problem may require an adjustment that is related to the point of valuation. For example, Figure A.14 also shows a five-year, $100 annuity. However, in this case, the first cash flow in the annuity does not occur until year 6. In addition, the point of valuation that is of interest in the problem is year 2. One possible scenario that might correspond with this time line is an investment that will return five payments that begin six years from now but return nothing in the earlier years. Furthermore, the investment may not be available or ready for investment for another two years. So the question is, "Given these are the future payments, what will they be worth two years from today?"

Applying the present value interest factor of an annuity to the $100 cash flows, that is, multiplying $100 by the PVIFA for the combination of 8 percent and five years, again produces the result of $399.27 (see also Figure A.11). Because of the rule with respect to implied point of valuation, this amount is the value of the annuity as of year 5 (one year before the first cash flow). Since the requirement is to determine the value as of year 2, this amount must be discounted for three years. The annuity effectively has been reduced to a single amount that is a valid estimate of value as of at year 5. At the same time, the problem at-hand requires valuation at year 2. Since there are three periods between the restated cash flow (year 5) and the point of valuation according to the scenario (year 2), n for the PVIF is 3. The value as of year 2 is $316.95.

These examples illustrate the use of both annuity and single amount factors as applicable. It should be remembered that the annuity factors have special interpretations of implied point of valuation and number of periods. With these stipulations in mind, the future value of an annuity may be expressed as:

$$FV = CF\ (FVIFA_{k,n}) \tag{8}$$

where $FVIFA_{k,n} = \left(\dfrac{(1 + k)^n - 1}{k}\right)$

The present value of an annuity can be expressed as:

$$PV = CF\ (PVIFA_{k,n}) \tag{9}$$

where $PVIFA_{k,n} = \left(\dfrac{1 - \dfrac{1}{(1 + k)^n}}{k} \right)$

FINANCIAL CALCULATORS

A number of hand-held calculators will perform the functions illustrated in this chapter for single amounts and annuities. In the case of a single amount, there are four variables that must be considered:

- number of periods
- interest rate
- present value
- future value.

Only one of these may be an unknown variable; three are entered into the calculator, the calculator is programmed to compute the fourth.

In the case of annuities, there are two possible combinations. In each case there are four variables. The first case is future value of an annuity and the variables are:

- interest rate
- number of periods
- payment
- future value.

The second case is present value of annuity and the variables are:

- interest rate
- number of periods
- payment
- present value.

Again, no more than one of these may be left as an unknown.

FIGURE A.15

Financial Calculator Example – Future Value of an Annuity

0	1	2	3	4	5	6	7	8
								*
	100	100	100	100	100			
								?

Keystroke		Display
f	FIN	[To clear previous entries.]
100	PMT	100.000000
8	i	8.000000
5	n	5.000000
	FV	–586.660096
f	FIN	–586.660096 [To clear.]
	PV	–586.660096
8	i	8.00000000
3	n	3.00000000
	FV	739.022763

Note: This example uses the Hewlett-Packard 12C. Other financial calculator applications will differ slightly depending on the model.

Figure A.15 illustrates the application of hand held calculator techniques for the problem previously illustrated in Figure A.13. It is a five-year $100 annuity at 8 percent that is to be valued as of year 8. The first step is to clear all registers of a calculator. Then the payment, interest rate, and number of payments are entered as shown. Once these three variables have been input, the command for calculation of future value is registered by pressing the FV key. Notice that the display will show the future value of $586.66. This is equivalent to the application of the future value interest factor of an annuity formula, which is the formula that financial calculators use. Notice that there is no indication on the calculator's display that this is a value as of year 5. Nevertheless, it coincides exactly with the previous calculations of FV$_5$. It is necessary for the user to understand this implied point of valuation. This completes the first half of the problem.

The second half of the problem is to value the annuity as of year 8. The $586.66 amount now becomes the present value. But before the calculation can be performed, the registers must be cleared once again. This part of the operation involves a single amount ($586.66) and will not require the use of the payment key. Instead, the amount of $586.66 is input as present value. The interest rate and number of periods are input and the command for future value registered. As found earlier, the future value is $739.02.

FIGURE A.16

Financial Calculator Example – Present Value of an Annuity

0	1	2	3	4	5	6	7	8	9	10
		*								
						100	100	100	100	100
		?								

Keystroke		Display
f	FIN	[To clear previous entries.]
100	PMT	100.000000
8	i	8.000000
5	n	5.000000
	PV	−399.271004
f	FIN	−399.271004 [To clear.]
	FV	−399.271004
8	i	8.00000000
3	n	3.00000000
	PV	316.954196

Note: This example uses the Hewlett-Packard 12C. Other financial calculator applications will differ slightly depending on the model.

The present value of the five-year, $100 annuity that begins in year 6 but must be valued as of year 2 is shown in Figure A.16, corresponding to the earlier example in Figure A.14. Again, the financial registers must be cleared. Once that has been done, the interest, number of periods, and payment are input. The command is registered for the present value of the annuity. The result is $399.27 as was the case in Figure A.14. The annuity problem has now been reduced to a single amount problem, completing the first half of the problem.

The registers are cleared once again and the $399.27 is input as the future value. The interest rate of 8 percent and the number of periods of three are input and the command for present value is registered. As was the case in the earlier calculation, the present value is $316.95.

Combinations of present value, future value, single amount, and annuities are easily accommodated on hand-held calculators with financial functions. However, the user must understand the nature of the calculations and the assumptions that have been built into the programming of such calculators.

It also should be noted that when future values are input either as single amounts or annuities, present values will be computed by financial calculators and associated with the opposite algebraic sign. Likewise, when present values are input, future values and annuities will be computed by the calculators and associated with the opposite algebraic sign. The reasoning for such programming is that it is illogical to both receive a future cash flow, that is, realize a positive cash flow in the future, and to receive a positive cash flow at the present time. This would be equivalent to suggesting that one could receive a cash payment today and also receive cash payments in the future. Instead, one either makes a payment today and receives payment in the future or vice versa.

This logic also follows when using financial calculators to compute an expected rate of return. In this case, the present value, future value (or amount of each future payment), and number of periods are input and the command is registered to find the interest rate. If both the present value and the future value (or amount of each future payment) have the same sign, an error message will generally be received.

SUMMARY OF TIME VALUE OF MONEY CONCEPTS

The time value of money is an important element in valuing mergers and acquisitions. It begins with a basic understanding of the premise that dollars received today are more valuable than dollars received in the future. The concepts also encompass measurement of rates of return for stated cash flows and valuation of multiple cash flow streams. There are a number of preprogrammed, hand-held calculators. In any event, the proper application of these concepts requires a clear understanding of the timing of actual cash flows and points of valuation (both implied and stated). Valuation in the context of mergers and acquisitions hinges on the appropriate application of these concepts.

PRESENT VALUE AND FUTURE VALUE FACTORS

Future Value of $1

■

Future Value of an Annuity of $1

■

Present Value of $1

■

Present Value of an Annuity of $1

Future Value of $1

$$FVIF = (1 + k)^n$$

Periods	1%	2%	3%	4%	5%	6%	7%	8%	9%	10%
1	1.0100	1.0200	1.0300	1.0400	1.0500	1.0600	1.0700	1.0800	1.0900	1.1000
2	1.0201	1.0404	1.0609	1.0816	1.1025	1.1236	1.1449	1.1664	1.1881	1.2100
3	1.0303	1.0612	1.0927	1.1249	1.1576	1.1910	1.2250	1.2597	1.2950	1.3310
4	1.0406	1.0824	1.1255	1.1699	1.2155	1.2625	1.3108	1.3605	1.4116	1.4641
5	1.0510	1.1041	1.1593	1.2167	1.2763	1.3382	1.4026	1.4693	1.5386	1.6105
6	1.0615	1.1262	1.1941	1.2653	1.3401	1.4185	1.5007	1.5869	1.6771	1.7716
7	1.0721	1.1487	1.2299	1.3159	1.4071	1.5036	1.6058	1.7138	1.8280	1.9487
8	1.0829	1.1717	1.2668	1.3686	1.4775	1.5938	1.7182	1.8509	1.9926	2.1436
9	1.0937	1.1951	1.3048	1.4233	1.5513	1.6895	1.8385	1.9990	2.1719	2.3579
10	1.1046	1.2190	1.3439	1.4802	1.6289	1.7908	1.9672	2.1589	2.3674	2.5937
11	1.1157	1.2434	1.3842	1.5395	1.7103	1.8983	2.1049	2.3316	2.5804	2.8531
12	1.1268	1.2682	1.4258	1.6010	1.7959	2.0122	2.2522	2.5182	2.8127	3.1384
13	1.1381	1.2936	1.4685	1.6651	1.8856	2.1329	2.4098	2.7196	3.0658	3.4523
14	1.1495	1.3195	1.5126	1.7317	1.9799	2.2609	2.5785	2.9372	3.3417	3.7975
15	1.1610	1.3459	1.5580	1.8009	2.0789	2.3966	2.7590	3.1722	3.6425	4.1772
16	1.1726	1.3728	1.6047	1.8730	2.1829	2.5404	2.9522	3.4259	3.9703	4.5950
17	1.1843	1.4002	1.6528	1.9479	2.2920	2.6928	3.1588	3.7000	4.3276	5.0545
18	1.1961	1.4282	1.7024	2.0258	2.4066	2.8543	3.3799	3.9960	4.7171	5.5599
19	1.2081	1.4568	1.7535	2.1068	2.5270	3.0256	3.6165	4.3157	5.1417	6.1159
20	1.2202	1.4859	1.8061	2.1911	2.6533	3.2071	3.8697	4.6610	5.6044	6.7275
25	1.2824	1.6406	2.0938	2.6658	3.3864	4.2919	5.4274	6.8485	8.6231	10.8347
30	1.3478	1.8114	2.4273	3.2434	4.3219	5.7435	7.6123	10.0627	13.2677	17.4494
35	1.4166	1.9999	2.8139	3.9461	5.5160	7.6861	10.6766	14.7853	20.4140	28.1024
40	1.4889	2.2080	3.2620	4.8010	7.0400	10.2857	14.9745	21.7245	31.4094	45.2593
45	1.5648	2.4379	3.7816	5.8412	8.9850	13.7646	21.0025	31.9204	48.3273	72.8905
50	1.6446	2.6916	4.3839	7.1067	11.4674	18.4202	29.4570	46.9016	74.3575	117.3909

11%	12%	13%	14%	15%	16%	17%	18%	19%	20%	Periods
1.1100	1.1200	1.1300	1.1400	1.1500	1.1600	1.1700	1.1800	1.1900	1.2000	1
1.2321	1.2544	1.2769	1.2996	1.3225	1.3456	1.3689	1.3924	1.4161	1.4400	2
1.3676	1.4049	1.4429	1.4815	1.5209	1.5609	1.6016	1.6430	1.6852	1.7280	3
1.5181	1.5735	1.6305	1.6890	1.7490	1.8106	1.8739	1.9388	2.0053	2.0736	4
1.6851	1.7623	1.8424	1.9254	2.0114	2.1003	2.1924	2.2878	2.3864	2.4883	5
1.8704	1.9738	2.0820	2.1950	2.3131	2.4364	2.5652	2.6996	2.8398	2.9860	6
2.0762	2.2107	2.3526	2.5023	2.6600	2.8262	3.0012	3.1855	3.3793	3.5832	7
2.3045	2.4760	2.6584	2.8526	3.0590	3.2784	3.5115	3.7589	4.0214	4.2998	8
2.5580	2.7731	3.0040	3.2519	3.5179	3.8030	4.1084	4.4355	4.7854	5.1598	9
2.8394	3.1058	3.3946	3.7072	4.0456	4.4114	4.8068	5.2338	5.6947	6.1917	10
3.1518	3.4785	3.8359	4.2262	4.6524	5.1173	5.6240	6.1759	6.7767	7.4301	11
3.4985	3.8960	4.3345	4.8179	5.3503	5.9360	6.5801	7.2876	8.0642	8.9161	12
3.8833	4.3635	4.8980	5.4924	6.1528	6.8858	7.6987	8.5994	9.5964	10.6993	13
4.3104	4.8871	5.5348	6.2613	7.0757	7.9875	9.0075	10.1472	11.4198	12.8392	14
4.7846	5.4736	6.2543	7.1379	8.1371	9.2655	10.5387	11.9737	13.5895	15.4070	15
5.3109	6.1304	7.0673	8.1372	9.3576	10.7480	12.3303	14.1290	16.1715	18.4884	16
5.8951	6.8660	7.9861	9.2765	10.7613	12.4677	14.4265	16.6722	19.2441	22.1861	17
6.5436	7.6900	9.0243	10.5752	12.3755	14.4625	16.8790	19.6733	22.9005	26.6233	18
7.2633	8.6128	10.1974	12.0557	14.2318	16.7765	19.7484	23.2144	27.2516	31.9480	19
8.0623	9.6463	11.5231	13.7435	16.3665	19.4608	23.1056	27.3930	32.4294	38.3376	20
13.5855	17.0001	21.2305	26.4619	32.9190	40.8742	50.6578	62.6686	77.3881	95.3962	25
22.8923	29.9599	39.1159	50.9502	66.2118	85.8499	111.0647	143.3706	184.6753	237.3763	30
38.5749	52.7996	72.0685	98.1002	133.1755	180.3141	243.5035	327.9973	440.7006	590.6682	35
65.0009	93.0510	132.7816	188.8835	267.8635	378.7212	533.8687	750.3783	1.05e+03	1.47e+03	40
109.5302	163.9876	244.6414	363.6791	538.7693	795.4438	1.17e+03	1.72e+03	2.51e+03	3.66e+03	45
184.5648	289.0022	450.7359	700.2330	1.08e+03	1.67e+03	2.57e+03	3.93e+03	5.99e+03	9.10e+03	50

Future Value of an Annuity of $1

$$\text{FVIFA} = [(1 + k)^n - 1]/k$$

Periods	1%	2%	3%	4%	5%	6%	7%	8%	9%	10%
1	1.0000	1.0000	1.0000	1.0000	1.0000	1.0000	1.0000	1.0000	1.0000	1.0000
2	2.0100	2.0200	2.0300	2.0400	2.0500	2.0600	2.0700	2.0800	2.0900	2.1000
3	3.0301	3.0604	3.0909	3.1216	3.1525	3.1836	3.2149	3.2464	3.2781	3.3100
4	4.0604	4.1216	4.1836	4.2465	4.3101	4.3746	4.4399	4.5061	4.5731	4.6410
5	5.1010	5.2040	5.3091	5.4163	5.5256	5.6371	5.7507	5.8666	5.9847	6.1051
6	6.1520	6.3081	6.4684	6.6330	6.8019	6.9753	7.1533	7.3359	7.5233	7.7156
7	7.2135	7.4343	7.6625	7.8983	8.1420	8.3938	8.6540	8.9228	9.2004	9.4872
8	8.2857	8.5830	8.8923	9.2142	9.5491	9.8975	10.2598	10.6366	11.0285	11.4359
9	9.3685	9.7546	10.1591	10.5828	11.0266	11.4913	11.9780	12.4876	13.0210	13.5795
10	10.4622	10.9497	11.4639	12.0061	12.5779	13.1808	13.8164	14.4866	15.1929	15.9374
11	11.5668	12.1687	12.8078	13.4864	14.2068	14.9716	15.7836	16.6455	17.5603	18.5312
12	12.6825	13.4121	14.1920	15.0258	15.9171	16.8699	17.8885	18.9771	20.1407	21.3843
13	13.8093	14.6803	15.6178	16.6268	17.7130	18.8821	20.1406	21.4953	22.9534	24.5227
14	14.9474	15.9739	17.0863	18.2919	19.5986	21.0151	22.5505	24.2149	26.0192	27.9750
15	16.0969	17.2934	18.5989	20.0236	21.5786	23.2760	25.1290	27.1521	29.3609	31.7725
16	17.2579	18.6393	20.1569	21.8245	23.6575	25.6725	27.8881	30.3243	33.0034	35.9497
17	18.4304	20.0121	21.7616	23.6975	25.8404	28.2129	30.8402	33.7502	36.9737	40.5447
18	19.6147	21.4123	23.4144	25.6454	28.1324	30.9057	33.9990	37.4502	41.3013	45.5992
19	20.8109	22.8406	25.1169	27.6712	30.5390	33.7600	37.3790	41.4463	46.0185	51.1591
20	22.0190	24.2974	26.8704	29.7781	33.0660	36.7856	40.9955	45.7620	51.1601	57.2750
25	28.2432	32.0303	36.4593	41.6459	47.7271	54.8645	63.2490	73.1059	84.7009	98.3471
30	34.7849	40.5681	47.5754	56.0849	66.4388	79.0582	94.4608	113.2832	136.3075	164.4940
35	41.6603	49.9945	60.4621	73.6522	90.3203	111.4348	138.2369	172.3168	215.7108	271.0244
40	48.8864	60.4020	75.4013	95.0255	120.7998	154.7620	199.6351	259.0565	337.8824	442.5926
45	56.4811	71.8927	92.7199	121.0294	159.7002	212.7435	285.7493	386.5056	525.8587	718.9048
50	64.4632	84.5794	112.7969	152.6671	209.3480	290.3359	406.5289	573.7702	815.0836	1.16e+03

11%	12%	13%	14%	15%	16%	17%	18%	19%	20%	Periods
1.0000	1.0000	1.0000	1.0000	1.0000	1.0000	1.0000	1.0000	1.0000	1.0000	1
2.1100	2.1200	2.1300	2.1400	2.1500	2.1600	2.1700	2.1800	2.1900	2.2000	2
3.3421	3.3744	3.4069	3.4396	3.4725	3.5056	3.5389	3.5724	3.6061	3.6400	3
4.7097	4.7793	4.8498	4.9211	4.9934	5.0665	5.1405	5.2154	5.2913	5.3680	4
6.2278	6.3528	6.4803	6.6101	6.7424	6.8771	7.0144	7.1542	7.2966	7.4416	5
7.9129	8.1152	8.3227	8.5355	8.7537	8.9775	9.2068	9.4420	9.6830	9.9299	6
9.7833	10.0890	10.4047	10.7305	11.0668	11.4139	11.7720	12.1415	12.5227	12.9159	7
11.8594	12.2997	12.7573	13.2328	13.7268	14.2401	14.7733	15.3270	15.9020	16.4991	8
14.1640	14.7757	15.4157	16.0853	16.7858	17.5185	18.2847	19.0859	19.9234	20.7989	9
16.7220	17.5487	18.4197	19.3373	20.3037	21.3215	22.3931	23.5213	24.7089	25.9587	10
19.5614	20.6546	21.8143	23.0445	24.3493	25.7329	27.1999	28.7551	30.4035	32.1504	11
22.7132	24.1331	25.6502	27.2707	29.0017	30.8502	32.8239	34.9311	37.1802	39.5805	12
26.2116	28.0291	29.9847	32.0887	34.3519	36.7862	39.4040	42.2187	45.2445	48.4966	13
30.0949	32.3926	34.8827	37.5811	40.5047	43.6720	47.1027	50.8180	54.8409	59.1959	14
34.4054	37.2797	40.4175	43.8424	47.5804	51.6595	56.1101	60.9653	66.2607	72.0351	15
39.1899	42.7533	46.6717	50.9804	55.7175	60.9250	66.6488	72.9390	79.8502	87.4421	16
44.5008	48.8837	53.7391	59.1176	65.0751	71.6730	78.9792	87.0680	96.0218	105.9306	17
50.3959	55.7497	61.7251	68.3941	75.8364	84.1407	93.4056	103.7403	115.2659	128.1167	18
56.9395	63.4397	70.7494	78.9692	88.2118	98.6032	110.2846	123.4135	138.1664	154.7400	19
64.2028	72.0524	80.9468	91.0249	102.4436	115.3797	130.0329	146.6280	165.4180	186.6880	20
114.4133	133.3339	155.6196	181.8708	212.7930	249.2140	292.1049	342.6035	402.0425	471.9811	25
199.0209	241.3327	293.1992	356.7868	434.7451	530.3117	647.4391	790.9480	966.7122	1.18e+03	30
341.5896	431.6635	546.6808	693.5727	881.1702	1.12e+03	1.43e+03	1.82e+03	2.31e+03	2.95e+03	35
581.8261	767.0914	1.01e+03	1.34e+03	1.78e+03	2.36e+03	3.13e+03	4.16e+03	5.53e+03	7.34e+03	40
986.6386	1.36e+03	1.87e+03	2.59e+03	3.59e+03	4.97e+03	6.88e+03	9.53e+03	1.32e+04	1.83e+04	45
1.67e+03	2.40e+03	3.46e+03	4.99e+03	7.22e+03	1.04e+04	1.51e+04	2.18e+04	3.15e+04	4.55e+04	50

Present Value of $1

$$PVIF = 1/(1+k)^n$$

Periods	1%	2%	3%	4%	5%	6%	7%	8%	9%	10%
1	0.9901	0.9804	0.9709	0.9615	0.9524	0.9434	0.9346	0.9259	0.9174	0.9091
2	0.9803	0.9612	0.9426	0.9246	0.9070	0.8900	0.8734	0.8573	0.8417	0.8264
3	0.9706	0.9423	0.9151	0.8890	0.8638	0.8396	0.8163	0.7938	0.7722	0.7513
4	0.9610	0.9238	0.8885	0.8548	0.8227	0.7921	0.7629	0.7350	0.7084	0.6830
5	0.9515	0.9057	0.8626	0.8219	0.7835	0.7473	0.7130	0.6806	0.6499	0.6209
6	0.9420	0.8880	0.8375	0.7903	0.7462	0.7050	0.6663	0.6302	0.5963	0.5645
7	0.9327	0.8706	0.8131	0.7599	0.7107	0.6651	0.6227	0.5835	0.5470	0.5132
8	0.9235	0.8535	0.7894	0.7307	0.6768	0.6274	0.5820	0.5403	0.5019	0.4665
9	0.9143	0.8368	0.7664	0.7026	0.6446	0.5919	0.5439	0.5002	0.4604	0.4241
10	0.9053	0.8203	0.7441	0.6756	0.6139	0.5584	0.5083	0.4632	0.4224	0.3855
11	0.8963	0.8043	0.7224	0.6496	0.5847	0.5268	0.4751	0.4289	0.3875	0.3505
12	0.8874	0.7885	0.7014	0.6246	0.5568	0.4970	0.4440	0.3971	0.3555	0.3186
13	0.8787	0.7730	0.6810	0.6006	0.5303	0.4688	0.4150	0.3677	0.3262	0.2897
14	0.8700	0.7579	0.6611	0.5775	0.5051	0.4423	0.3878	0.3405	0.2992	0.2633
15	0.8613	0.7430	0.6419	0.5553	0.4810	0.4173	0.3624	0.3152	0.2745	0.2394
16	0.8528	0.7284	0.6232	0.5339	0.4581	0.3936	0.3387	0.2919	0.2519	0.2176
17	0.8444	0.7142	0.6050	0.5134	0.4363	0.3714	0.3166	0.2703	0.2311	0.1978
18	0.8360	0.7002	0.5874	0.4936	0.4155	0.3503	0.2959	0.2502	0.2120	0.1799
19	0.8277	0.6864	0.5703	0.4746	0.3957	0.3305	0.2765	0.2317	0.1945	0.1635
20	0.8195	0.6730	0.5537	0.4564	0.3769	0.3118	0.2584	0.2145	0.1784	0.1486
25	0.7798	0.6095	0.4776	0.3751	0.2953	0.2330	0.1842	0.1460	0.1160	0.0923
30	0.7419	0.5521	0.4120	0.3083	0.2314	0.1741	0.1314	0.0994	0.0754	0.0573
35	0.7059	0.5000	0.3554	0.2534	0.1813	0.1301	0.0937	0.0676	0.0490	0.0356
40	0.6717	0.4529	0.3066	0.2083	0.1420	0.0972	0.0668	0.0460	0.0318	0.0221
45	0.6391	0.4102	0.2644	0.1712	0.1113	0.0727	0.0476	0.0313	0.0207	0.0137
50	1.0000	0.3715	0.2281	0.1407	0.0872	0.0543	0.0339	0.0213	0.0134	0.0085

11%	12%	13%	14%	15%	16%	17%	18%	19%	20%	Periods
0.9009	0.8929	0.8850	0.8772	0.8696	0.8621	0.8547	0.8475	0.8403	0.8333	1
0.8116	0.7972	0.7831	0.7695	0.7561	0.7432	0.7305	0.7182	0.7062	0.6944	2
0.7312	0.7118	0.6931	0.6750	0.6575	0.6407	0.6244	0.6086	0.5934	0.5787	3
0.6587	0.6355	0.6133	0.5921	0.5718	0.5523	0.5337	0.5158	0.4987	0.4823	4
0.5935	0.5674	0.5428	0.5194	0.4972	0.4761	0.4561	0.4371	0.4190	0.4019	5
0.5346	0.5066	0.4803	0.4556	0.4323	0.4104	0.3898	0.3704	0.3521	0.3349	6
0.4817	0.4523	0.4251	0.3996	0.3759	0.3538	0.3332	0.3139	0.2959	0.2791	7
0.4339	0.4039	0.3762	0.3506	0.3269	0.3050	0.2848	0.2660	0.2487	0.2326	8
0.3909	0.3606	0.3329	0.3075	0.2843	0.2630	0.2434	0.2255	0.2090	0.1938	9
0.3522	0.3220	0.2946	0.2697	0.2472	0.2267	0.2080	0.1911	0.1756	0.1615	10
0.3173	0.2875	0.2607	0.2366	0.2149	0.1954	0.1778	0.1619	0.1476	0.1346	11
0.2858	0.2567	0.2307	0.2076	0.1869	0.1685	0.1520	0.1372	0.1240	0.1122	12
0.2575	0.2292	0.2042	0.1821	0.1625	0.1452	0.1299	0.1163	0.1042	0.0935	13
0.2320	0.2046	0.1807	0.1597	0.1413	0.1252	0.1110	0.0985	0.0876	0.0779	14
0.2090	0.1827	0.1599	0.1401	0.1229	0.1079	0.0949	0.0835	0.0736	0.0649	15
0.1883	0.1631	0.1415	0.1229	0.1069	0.0930	0.0811	0.0708	0.0618	0.0541	16
0.1696	0.1456	0.1252	0.1078	0.0929	0.0802	0.0693	0.0600	0.0520	0.0451	17
0.1528	0.1300	0.1108	0.0946	0.0808	0.0691	0.0592	0.0508	0.0437	0.0376	18
0.1377	0.1161	0.0981	0.0829	0.0703	0.0596	0.0506	0.0431	0.0367	0.0313	19
0.1240	0.1037	0.0868	0.0728	0.0611	0.0514	0.0433	0.0365	0.0308	0.0261	20
0.0736	0.0588	0.0471	0.0378	0.0304	0.0245	0.0197	0.0160	0.0129	0.0105	25
0.0437	0.0334	0.0256	0.0196	0.0151	0.0116	0.0090	0.0070	0.0054	0.0042	30
0.0259	0.0189	0.0139	0.0102	0.0075	0.0055	0.0041	0.0030	0.0023	0.0017	35
0.0154	0.0107	0.0075	0.0053	0.0037	0.0026	0.0019	0.0013	0.0010	0.0007	40
0.0091	0.0061	0.0041	0.0027	0.0019	0.0013	0.0009	0.0006	0.0004	0.0003	45
0.0054	0.0035	0.0022	0.0014	0.0009	0.0006	0.0004	0.0003	0.0002	0.0001	50

Present Value of an Annuity of $1

$$PVIFA = [1-1/(1+k)^n]/k$$

Periods	1%	2%	3%	4%	5%	6%	7%	8%	9%	10%
1	0.9901	0.9804	0.9709	0.9615	0.9524	0.9434	0.9346	0.9259	0.9174	0.9091
2	1.9704	1.9416	1.9135	1.8861	1.8594	1.8334	1.8080	1.7833	1.7591	1.7355
3	2.9410	2.8839	2.8286	2.7751	2.7232	2.6730	2.6243	2.5771	2.5313	2.4869
4	3.9020	3.8077	3.7171	3.6299	3.5460	3.4651	3.3872	3.3121	3.2397	3.1699
5	4.8534	4.7135	4.5797	4.4518	4.3295	4.2124	4.1002	3.9927	3.8897	3.7908
6	5.7955	5.6014	5.4172	5.2421	5.0757	4.9173	4.7665	4.6229	4.4859	4.3553
7	6.7282	6.4720	6.2303	6.0021	5.7864	5.5824	5.3893	5.2064	5.0330	4.8684
8	7.6517	7.3255	7.0197	6.7327	6.4632	6.2098	5.9713	5.7466	5.5348	5.3349
9	8.5660	8.1622	7.7861	7.4353	7.1078	6.8017	6.5152	6.2469	5.9952	5.7590
10	9.4713	8.9826	8.5302	8.1109	7.7217	7.3601	7.0236	6.7101	6.4177	6.1446
11	10.3676	9.7868	9.2526	8.7605	8.3064	7.8869	7.4987	7.1390	6.8052	6.4951
12	11.2551	10.5753	9.9540	9.3851	8.8633	8.3838	7.9427	7.5361	7.1607	6.8137
13	12.1337	11.3484	10.6350	9.9856	9.3936	8.8527	8.3577	7.9038	7.4869	7.1034
14	13.0037	12.1062	11.2961	10.5631	9.8986	9.2950	8.7455	8.2442	7.7862	7.3667
15	13.8651	12.8493	11.9379	11.1184	10.3797	9.7122	9.1079	8.5595	8.0607	7.6061
16	14.7179	13.5777	12.5611	11.6523	10.8378	10.1059	9.4466	8.8514	8.3126	7.8237
17	15.5623	14.2919	13.1661	12.1657	11.2741	10.4773	9.7632	9.1216	8.5436	8.0216
18	16.3983	14.9920	13.7535	12.6593	11.6896	10.8276	10.0591	9.3719	8.7556	8.2014
19	17.2260	15.6785	14.3238	13.1339	12.0853	11.1581	10.3356	9.6036	8.9501	8.3649
20	18.0456	16.3514	14.8775	13.5903	12.4622	11.4699	10.5940	9.8181	9.1285	8.5136
25	22.0232	19.5235	17.4131	15.6221	14.0939	12.7834	11.6536	10.6748	9.8226	9.0770
30	25.8077	22.3965	19.6004	17.2920	15.3725	13.7648	12.4090	11.2578	10.2737	9.4269
35	29.4086	24.9986	21.4872	18.6646	16.3742	14.4982	12.9477	11.6546	10.5668	9.6442
40	32.8347	27.3555	23.1148	19.7928	17.1591	15.0463	13.3317	11.9246	10.7574	9.7791
45	36.0945	29.4902	24.5187	20.7200	17.7741	15.4558	13.6055	12.1084	10.8812	9.8628
50	39.1961	31.4236	25.7298	21.4822	18.2559	15.7619	13.8007	12.2335	10.9617	9.9148

Present Value And Future Value Factors

11%	12%	13%	14%	15%	16%	17%	18%	19%	20%	Periods
0.9009	0.8929	0.8850	0.8772	0.8696	0.8621	0.8547	0.8475	0.8403	0.8333	1
1.7125	1.6901	1.6681	1.6467	1.6257	1.6052	1.5852	1.5656	1.5465	1.5278	2
2.4437	2.4018	2.3612	2.3216	2.2832	2.2459	2.2096	2.1743	2.1399	2.1065	3
3.1024	3.0373	2.9745	2.9137	2.8550	2.7982	2.7432	2.6901	2.6386	2.5887	4
3.6959	3.6048	3.5172	3.4331	3.3522	3.2743	3.1993	3.1272	3.0576	2.9906	5
4.2305	4.1114	3.9975	3.8887	3.7845	3.6847	3.5892	3.4976	3.4098	3.3255	6
4.7122	4.5638	4.4226	4.2883	4.1604	4.0386	3.9224	3.8115	3.7057	3.6046	7
5.1461	4.9676	4.7988	4.6389	4.4873	4.3436	4.2072	4.0776	3.9544	3.8372	8
5.5370	5.3282	5.1317	4.9464	4.7716	4.6065	4.4506	4.3030	4.1633	4.0310	9
5.8892	5.6502	5.4262	5.2161	5.0188	4.8332	4.6586	4.4941	4.3389	4.1925	10
6.2065	5.9377	5.6869	5.4527	5.2337	5.0286	4.8364	4.6560	4.4865	4.3271	11
6.4924	6.1944	5.9176	5.6603	5.4206	5.1971	4.9884	4.7932	4.6105	4.4392	12
6.7499	6.4235	6.1218	5.8424	5.5831	5.3423	5.1183	4.9095	4.7147	4.5327	13
6.9819	6.6282	6.3025	6.0021	5.7245	5.4675	5.2293	5.0081	4.8023	4.6106	14
7.1909	6.8109	6.4624	6.1422	5.8474	5.5755	5.3242	5.0916	4.8759	4.6755	15
7.3792	6.9740	6.6039	6.2651	5.9542	5.6685	5.4053	5.1624	4.9377	4.7296	16
7.5488	7.1196	6.7291	6.3729	6.0472	5.7487	5.4746	5.2223	4.9897	4.7746	17
7.7016	7.2497	6.8399	6.4674	6.1280	5.8178	5.5339	5.2732	5.0333	4.8122	18
7.8393	7.3658	6.9380	6.5504	6.1982	5.8775	5.5845	5.3162	5.0700	4.8435	19
7.9633	7.4694	7.0248	6.6231	6.2593	5.9288	5.6278	5.3527	5.1009	4.8696	20
8.4217	7.8431	7.3300	6.8729	6.4641	6.0971	5.7662	5.4669	5.1951	4.9476	25
8.6938	8.0552	7.4957	7.0027	6.5660	6.1772	5.8294	5.5168	5.2347	4.9789	30
8.8552	8.1755	7.5856	7.0700	6.6166	6.2153	5.8582	5.5386	5.2512	4.9915	35
8.9511	8.2438	7.6344	7.1050	6.6418	6.2335	5.8713	5.5482	5.2582	4.9966	40
9.0079	8.2825	7.6609	7.1232	6.6543	6.2421	5.8773	5.5523	5.2611	4.9986	45
9.0417	8.3045	7.6752	7.1327	6.6605	6.2463	5.8801	5.5541	5.2623	4.9995	50

INDEX

FIRM VALUATION SOFTWARE SYSTEM
(INTERACTIVE VERSION)

© Hazel J. Johnson 1999
Software Development Consultant: Derrick M. Johnson

Introduction

Firm Valuation Software System is an Excel 7.0-based system that facilitates a discounted cash flow (DCF) valuation of a commercial enterprise. The system can be used for a commercial or industrial firm as the categories are generalized. Cash flows are projected for a five-year period and a terminal value is then estimated that captures the value of cash flows after the forecasted period. The system is organized in a workbook format. Individual worksheets are devoted to specific aspects of company cash flows and valuation.

- Firm Identification
- Revenue Projections
- Cash Expense Projections
- Working Capital Changes
- Projected Capital Expenditures
- Noncash Expense Projections
- Cash Flow Summary
- Valuation Summary.

Each worksheet requires input from the user as indicated by a cell address in parentheses. For example,

Name of Firm (F6)

means that the user should place the name of the company being analyzed in cell F6.

Other line items are accompanied with the phrase "do not input." In these cases, the system is programmed to produce the result. No user input is required.

For most of the worksheets, growth rates are required – by category – for each of the next five years. In addition, the user is asked to estimate a long-run, sustainable growth rate for each category for year 6 and forward. These estimates of annual growth rates should be input in decimal (not percentage) form. For example, a 10 percent estimated growth rate should be input as 0.10.

USER'S MANUAL

System Installation

To install Firm Valuation Software System, save F_Val.xls on a hard drive with at least 500 kb of available disk space.

The Firm Valuation Software System should be placed on the user's hard drive. In this way, should any of the code be erased inadvertently, the diskette version of the program can be used to reinstall the system.

System Operation

On the Windows task bar, press the "Start" button. Choose "run." In the dialogue box, type the full path name of the file, for example,

c:\firmval\f_val.xls

where c:\firmval is the path of the file. The first worksheet will appear – "Firm."

Manual Mode

To use the system as a regular spreadsheet, input the information requested in cells F6, F8, F10, F12, and F20 of "Firm." Proceed to the next sheet, by clicking the tab at the bottom of the spreadsheet – "Revenue." Input the requested information. Continue this process through the following sheets:

- Cash_Expenses
- Working_Capital
- Capital_Assets
- Noncash_Expenses
- Cash_Flows
- Valuation.

Interactive Mode

Click the "Main Menu" button on the "Firm" worksheet.

- To enter all data via text boxes and have the information automatically placed in the appropriate cell:

  – select "Interactive Mode;"

- press the "Next" button;
- enter name of firm, date of valuation, cost of capital (decimal form), marginal income tax rate (decimal form), and name of analyst;
- use the tab key to move from one text box to the next text box;
- continue the input as requested;
- the "Exit" button will terminate the Interactive Mode and place the cursor in the last field of input.

- To return to the Manual Mode, select "Manual Mode" and press "Next."

The following sections describe the specific data required in each case.

Firm Identification

Data required:

- name of the firm to be valued;
- date of the valuation;
- weighted average cost of capital of the firm to be valued (in decimal form);
- marginal corporate income tax rate of the firm to be valued (in decimal form).

Revenue Projections

Projected positive cash flows are based on the most recent annual results. The categories of revenue include:

- Sales of raw materials
- Sales of intermediate goods
- Sales of finished goods
- Fees for services
- Interest income from investments or subsidiaries
- Dividend income from investments or subsidiaries
- Other revenue.

In the manual mode, the most recently realized revenue amounts should be input in the appropriate cells of column F, as indicated. (The total is

USER'S MANUAL

automatically calculated and, thus, need not be input.) Below the revenue amounts, projected (estimated) growth rates should be input for each of the next five years as well as a sixth, long-run, sustainable growth rate. Growth rates are required for each category of revenue.

All of these categories may not be applicable. The amounts for any category that is not relevant should be left blank. Likewise, the growth rates for such categories should be left blank.

In the interactive mode, the user is prompted to provide all the above-mentioned information.

Cash Expense Projections

Amounts and growth rates of cash expenses are required on this worksheet. The following categories are provided:

- Cost of sales:
  - Materials
  - Labor
  - Overheads
  - Other cost of sales

- Personnel expenses:
  - Officers' salaries
  - Management salaries
  - Associate salaries
  - Other salaries and wages
  - Payroll tax expense
  - Employee health benefits
  - Life insurance benefits
  - Pension benefits
  - Management insurance
  - Other personnel expense

- Facilities expenses:
  - Building rental expense

- Building maintenance
- Equipment rental expense
- Equipment maintenance
- Utilities expense
- Telecommunications expense
- Property tax expense
- Facilities insurance expense
- Other facilities expense

■ Advertising expense

■ Vehicles expense

■ Travel and entertainment

■ Business licenses

■ Legal fees

■ Other professional fees

■ Supplies expense

■ Miscellaneous expense.

In manual mode, the current amount of these cash expenses should be input in column F. Input for corresponding annual growth rates begins in row 62.

In interactive mode, the user is asked first to input the current dollar amounts in each category. Then growth rate information is requested by category. That is, all the growth rates are requested for cost of sales – years 1 through 5 plus long-run. Then the same growth-rate information is requested for personnel expenses and so on.

Working Capital Changes

Any projected changes in working capital levels will have an impact on cash flow. The user should include these changes in the appropriate line or text box under the appropriate categories – current assets or current liabilities. The working capital line items are:

■ Cash
■ Accounts receivable

- Inventory
- Prepaid expenses
- Other current assets
- Accounts payable
- Accruals
- Deferred tax
- Other current liabilities.

In manual mode, current amounts should be placed in column F, with input for corresponding growth rates beginning in row 31.

In interactive mode, users are prompted to provide the dollar amounts of current expenses. Next growth rate information is requested.

Projected Capital Expenditures

Changes in the level of capital investment will also have an impact on cash flows. The treatment is comparable to changes in working capital. The categories of capital assets are:

- Land
- Buildings
- Equipment.

In manual mode, amounts are recorded in column F and annual growth rates input begins in row 25. In interactive mode, appropriate text boxes appear.

Noncash Expense Projections

Depreciation and amortization expense have no direct impact on cash flow. However, these amounts are tax deductible and are, thus, associated with tax savings. This worksheet captures the current amounts of depreciation and amortization as well as the anticipated annual growth rates. The classifications are:

- Building depreciation
- Equipment depreciation

- Amortization of goodwill
- Amortization of patents
- Amortization of copyrights
- Other noncash expenses.

In manual mode, amounts are input in column F with growth rate input starting in row 30. In interactive mode, appropriate text boxes appear.

Cash Flow Summary

The system automatically accumulates cash flow information from the preceding worksheets. The growth rates are used to project cash flows for the next six years. As applicable, the following tax adjustments are made.

- Revenues are multiplied by the factor $(1 - t)$, where t is the marginal corporate tax rate included in the "Firm" worksheet.
- Cash expenses are also multiplied by the factor $(1 - t)$.
- Year-end balances of working capital are automatically computed to determine anticipated changes in working capital.
- Year-end balances of capital assets are, likewise, used to estimate anticipated changes in asset levels.
- The amount of total noncash expenses is the basis for the depreciation tax shield in each of the forecasted years. The tax shield is calculated as the amount of depreciation multiplied by the marginal income tax rate, t.

No input by user is required.

Valuation Summary

Based on results in the Valuation Summary, this worksheet automatically computes:

- discounted cash flows (present value) for years 1 through 5;
- the value of estimated cash flows beyond year 5;
- the **value of the firm – in cell B23.**

No input is required by user.

USER'S MANUAL